9-27-07

To Dorothy,

May this be a gift of encouragement in your great journey. Peace —

Howard

A Dream That Came to Life: A History of Laity Lodge Retreat Center

Howard Hovde
Director Emeritus of Laity Lodge

Howard Hovde

Smyth & Helwys Publishing, Inc.
6316 Peake Road
Macon, Georgia 31210-3960
1-800-747-3016
©2007 by Smyth & Helwys Publishing

The paper used in this publication meets the minimum requirements of
American National Standard for Information Sciences—
Permanence of Paper for Printed Library Materials.
ANSI Z39.48–1984. (alk. paper)

Library of Congress Cataloging-in-Publication Data

Hovde, Howard.
A dream that came to life : the history of Laity Lodge retreat center / By
Howard Hovde.
p. cm.
Includes bibliographical references and index.
ISBN 978-1-57312-487-4 (pbk. : alk. paper)
1. Laity Lodge (Texas) 2. Spiritual retreat centers—Texas. 3. Spiritual
retreats—Christianity. I. Title.

BV5068.R4H67 2007
267'.13—dc22
2007001641

Contents

Chapter 9
Memories of the Dream: Testimonies from Laity Lodge

Chapter 10
The Future of the Dream

Foreword

"I'm just a layperson."

This sentence is usually spoken in the same self-deprecating inflection as "I'm just a homemaker" or "I've never been to seminary" or "Who am I that I should go to Pharaoh . . ." (Moses in Exod 3:11) or "I'm only a boy" (Jeremiah in Jer 1:7). It is an age-old habit, endemic to the human condition—if we don't have a socially sanctioned role, or a professionally certified position, or a recognized position in a family or community hierarchy, we feel inadequate and apologetic. As ourselves, just as ourselves, we have no "standing." Just as ourselves, we are *just* laypersons.

Meanwhile, at a retreat center in the Texas Hill Country, that "laity myth" is, week after week and year after year, exposed as the lie that it is. It only takes a few hours at Laity Lodge for the term to get scrubbed of every and any hint of condescension. "Laity" is restored to its gospel vigor. "Laity" is a term of dignity that Christian men and women are bold to carry with them into workplace and marketplace, home, and church without deference, without apology. They discover, not in a book or lecture, but in the way they are accepted and treated, that in the vocabulary of Scripture, they are the *people* of God (*laos*=people in the Greek Bible), capable just as they are, as able as Mary and Elizabeth, Peter, and John to hear, obey, love, and help "in Jesus' name."

Howard Hovde, Director Emeritus of Laity Lodge, gives us a detailed account of how this all came about, how it continues to be done, and stories of the people who are doing it—stories that are being replicated all over the world by laypersons who have recovered their gospel identity.

Within the Christian community, few words are more disabling than "layperson" and "laity." The words convey the impression—an impression that quickly solidifies into a lie—that there is a two-level hierarchy among the men and women who follow Jesus: those who are trained, sometimes referred to as "called," the professionals who are paid to preach, teach, and provide guidance in the Christian way, occupy the upper level; the lower level is made up of everyone else, those who are assigned jobs as storekeepers, lawyers, journalists, parents, and computer programmers.

It is a barefaced lie insinuated into the Christian community by the devil (who has an established reputation for using perfectly good words for telling lies). It is a lie because it misleads a huge company of Christians into assuming that their workplace severely limits their usefulness in the cause of Christ, that it necessarily confines them to part-time work for Jesus as they help out on the margins of God's kingdom work.

It is not difficult to account for this pervasive "laity" put-down among us. After all, we spend our most impressionable years smaller, weaker, less knowledgeable, more inexperienced than most of the people with whom we grow up. Is it any wonder that we carry these feelings of inadequacy into our adult lives? We commonly compensate by getting academic degrees, professional certification, awards, and trophies that are evidence of accomplishment; or we join a club, follow a guru, buy a late-model car, dress in the latest fashion, wear a cap that connects us with an athletic team. We acquire significance by taking on a role that defines our place in society or performing a function that is rewarded with money. What others think of us and how much they pay us go a long way in disguising feelings of inadequacy from our friends, our neighbors, and our fellow workers. There is at least one area of life in which we are not "just a layperson." If I am a mechanic I know more about the car you drive than you do. If I am a physician I know more about the body you inhabit than you do. If I am an English professor I know more about the language you speak than you do. And on and on and on.

But in the company of Christians, that simply doesn't work. On reflection, it is difficult to understand how the term "laity" and the assumptions drawn from it continue to marginalize so many Christians from all-out participation in Christ's work. Laity Lodge is one of the strategic places in the world where those assumptions are effectively challenged and disposed of. After all, didn't Jesus call only laypersons to follow him? Not a priest or professor among the twelve men and the numerous women followers. And Paul the tentmaker.

And David. The David story is the single most extensively narrated story in the entire biblical account. We know more about David than any other person in Holy Scripture. And David, most significantly, is a layperson. His life is not given to us under the forms of a role or function. It is not an accumulation of abstractions such as love and truth, sin and salvation, atonement and holiness, vision statements, and statistical measurements.

The way David's story is told is the way we learn to tell our stories—not in terms of who we know or the position we hold or the jobs we perform or the money we make, but in a realization of the details that connect organically in us, personally and specifically: names and fingerprints, street numbers and local weather, the casserole for supper and the flat tire in the rain. We get a feel for the *lived* dimensions of faith not through a metaphysical formulation or a cosmic fireworks display but in the kinds of stories we use to tell our children who they are and how to grow up as human beings, tell our friends who we are and what it is like to be human. These obscure details turn out to be pivotal, subtle accents of color and form and scent that give texture to our actions and feelings, give coherence to our meetings and relationships in workplace and family kitchen, locate our precise place in the neighborhood. As in the David story. As in the Jesus story. All the sharp-edged, fresh-minted details, but also the substrata of meaning and purpose and design implicit in all the details, small and large accorded equal dignity and linked together in an easy camaraderie. But to learn to tell our stories this way requires men and women who know how to listen to them in such terms. Laity Lodge people know how to listen. Apart from the world of role and function, often imposed as much in the church as in the world, Laity Lodge provides a spacious and unhurried community in which so many of us continue to recover our basic relational identity with one another and our very personal God.

The fact is that most people who venture upon a life of faith are laypersons. Why do so many of us habitually and pliantly take a subordinate position under the certified experts in matters of faith? As a pastor myself, I've never quite gotten over my surprise—!—at being treated with doggish deference by so many people. Where do all these Christians, who by definition are "new creatures in Christ" and therefore surely eager to taste and see for themselves (a universal characteristic in newborns) that the Lord is good, pick up this deprecating self-understanding? They certainly don't get it from the Bible or from the gospel. They get it from the culture, whether secular or ecclesial. They get it from leaders who love the prerogatives and power of expertise and bully people by means of their glamorous bravado into abdicating the original splendor of a new life in Christ and then declining into the wretched condition of the consumer. The consumer is passivity objectified: passive in the pew, passive before the TV screen, vulnerable to every sort of exploitation and seduction whether religious or secular.

Laity Lodge's first director, Keith Miller, forty-three years ago planted a seed in me. I was a newly ordained pastor at the time, and that seed quickly matured into a lifelong determination to do whatever I can to abolish this expert/layperson division in the Christian community. The company of people at Laity Lodge with remarkable consistency and energy continue to nurture that determination not only in me but in many, many others.

Eugene H. Peterson
Professor Emeritus of Spiritual Theology
Regent College
Vancouver, B.C.

Acknowledgments

I am grateful to Howard and Barbara Dan Butt for offering Carole and me the opportunity to give a major part of our working life to Laity Lodge. They are an inspiration to us and have been a constant source of encouragement. They are our mentors.

Eddie Sears is a dear friend and was a special colleague in the whole journey at Laity Lodge. Eddie helped make work a delight. Ila Burnett, my administrative assistant, was my wise counselor in our work and a thoughtful colleague in meeting the challenges of Laity Lodge. Georganne Grosbeck and Ann Jack picked up the mantle, and Ann continues to carry it. Mary Kalbfleisch brought her organizational and professional gifts as a nurse to transform the office and work of the hostesses. In addition, she trained many of us in basic first aid. Dwight Lacy, Dorothy Parish, Sam Fore, and Frances Worley were on the staff as we began and were helpful partners and caring friends.

The foundation staff members in Kerrville and in the canyon have grown to be friends. Maintenance, housekeeping, foodservice personnel, and hostesses are all a part of this work. Being a part of the ministry of the "Refreshment Stand by the Frio" with these friends has made life more beautiful for Carole and me.

The other Laity Lodge directors—Keith Miller, Bill Cody, Bill Huth, Eddie Sears, Don Murdock, and David Williamson—each helped make Laity Lodge a place God used to shape and change lives. I think of each individual as a good friend. They also brought their personal leadership gifts and thoughtful insights that make Laity Lodge an avenue of opening for the Spirit of God.

The awesome array of speakers, musicians, witnesses, and artists called us forth toward life with God.

I feel deep gratitude to our dear friend John Claypool for introducing us to Laity Lodge by inviting me to share in leading a retreat and, then, recommending us to Howard Butt Jr. when Howard was looking for a new director.

The retreat participants brought a world of wisdom, devotion, seeking, questioning, joy, and gratitude that brightened the world and brought life-giving gifts of the Spirit to Carole and me.

A special note of thanks is due those who have written from their experiences and heart-wisdom to enhance the telling of the Laity Lodge story: Keith Miller, Betty Anne Cody, Chuck Huffman, Jack Willome, Ralph and Jenny Berkeley, Robert and Lillian Morris, Norma Duff, Robert Sohn, Ginger Geyer, Hugh Schneeman, Glenn Echols, Don Murdock, David Williamson, Linda Worden, Eddie Sears, Dan Roloff, Jennifer Hargrave, Kathy Bort, Linda Hortness, Dora Canales, Tom Kingery, Guy Parker, Rebecca Lawson, Kevin Mayne and the Youth Camp staff, Lyn DeVille, and Cyra Dumitru. Keith Mirrer gave wise counsel on the whole project.

Marcus Goodyear, research and content editor for the H. E. Butt Foundation, brought his experience and editing skills to improve the quality of the writing.

Vickie Berry kept up with a wide variety of changes in the whole editing process to keep refining the work.

Laura Stott Williams used her unique skills as an editor as she worked her own kind of magic on the manuscript.

Leslie Williams has added her wisdom and professional editing gifts and has personally encouraged me. The work would not have emerged without her. Jane Miller gave expert counsel regarding both structure and style. She did all the necessary things to prepare the manuscript for publication.

I am especially grateful to Carole for fifty years of life together in a friendship and working partnership that has far exceeded anything I could have ever imagined. She carefully read the manuscript and made many valuable suggestions. And a word of deep appreciation to our children, Anna and John, and their families for the great joy they have brought us and the things they have taught us.

To Carole, my wife, with whom the Great Journey has grown continually deeper and more beautiful in life with Jesus Christ.

Introduction

Some places and experiences call to us, and we look for ways to follow those deep urgings and walk into a richer life. For more than eighteen years I worked in the Frio River Canyon at a place where God beckoned people to transform their lives. That place is Laity Lodge. Like the Frio River, a strong current of speakers, musicians, and artists flowed through this canyon in the Texas Hill Country. These men and women shared both the gentle light and poignant darkness of their lives. They provided spiritual rejuvenation to other guests who sought a closer relationship to God.

The Spirit draws pilgrims there. Holy unrest prompts many to go on a retreat. Laity Lodge, then, provides space and time to be open to God. It helps people rediscover a passion for our loving, present Savior. James Stewart, a Scottish cleric, described life with Christ as the happiest, hardest, holiest, and most hopeful life of all. At Laity Lodge, many people make decisions to begin the journey toward this kind of life. Many choose to deepen their lives through study of the Bible, through a more focused life of prayer, through more intentional work, or through intensified family and community life. Many people learn about Christ's transforming power and servant leadership. Nearly all who come to Laity Lodge discover a safe place to seek deeper relationships with God, their families, and their work.

What makes Laity Lodge such a safe yet challenging place? In the pages that follow, we will go on a grand adventure to answer that question. We will hear the stories of the H. E. Butt family and many others, through whom God provided the vision, passion, and faith that brought Laity Lodge into being.

Wilford Peterson writes, "A man practices the art of adventure when he breaks the chain of routine and renews his life through reading new books, traveling to new places, making new friends, taking up new hobbies and adopting new viewpoints." As we read about the hosts of Laity Lodge and the guests who met with God there, we will practice the art of adventure. May we, too, "hear deep calling unto deep" (Ps 42:7). May all his waves and breakers sweep over us.

Note

1 Wilferd Peterson. *Distilled Wisdom.* Ed. A. A. Montapert (Englewood Cliffs, NJ: Prentice-Hall, 1964) 8.

Chapter 1

Why the Dream: Does Your Heart Long for Rest?

Blessed are they who are glad to have time to spare for God.[1]

A Sense of Emptiness

He was old and felt driven to talk with someone. He had opened up to one friend and knew the friend hadn't heard him. He sought a counselor because he needed a listening ear. Not answers. Not advice.

For the past three weeks, he had been robbed of sleep. He remembered his high school and college graduations, when he first asked himself the question, "What are you going to do?" After high school, he had known the answer. He would go to a university. After the university, he had known he would go to work. Selling was natural for him. He bought a modest house, purchased used cars to travel close to home, and gave his time to a social club. He served on committees and did two terms as president. People liked him, and he cherished their friendships.

Now he was seventy-two and sleepless. His company had awarded him a watch for thirty-eight years of service. Tonight, like every night, it lay nestled on the gray cloth that covered his chest of drawers, keeping time for the empty room.

"I have given my life to the wrong things," the man had said to his counselor. His life had not been bad. Nor sordid. Nor unacceptable to the community. Only empty.

A thirty-five-year-old philosophy student-turned-salesman experienced a similar lack of meaning in life. He said, "I know what time I will get up, what I'll have for breakfast, what traffic lanes I'll drive in, where I'll park, the time the boss will come through to check on the sales for the morning, the time I'll take a break for lunch, where I will eat and even what I'll have, the time I'll leave and which path I'll take going home." He concluded, "If this is life, I don't want it."

The Search for Meaning

We all need time to ask the big life questions. What did I do with the gifts God has given me? What is the purpose of my life? The Presbyterian Catechism says we are here to "worship God and to enjoy him forever." William Blake wrote, "We are put on earth a little space / that we may learn to bear the beams of love."[2] When we look back on our lives, will we see deeply satisfying memories or dull and empty pictures?

An astute lawyer had just returned from his father's funeral, and we stood in the parking lot outside my office. The conversation turned somber. "I bet there were a hundred and fifty people who came by to tell me how much my father had meant to them. If I died today, I don't know of anyone who would say that about me," he said. Then that big man began to weep. "I don't want the bottom line of my life to be, 'He saved the company a million dollars.'"[3]

I read a story several years ago about a married couple. Both husband and wife were successful in business. The husband founded a profitable technology company. The wife managed hardware products for a major computer brand. They shared a passion for sports as well (both were triathletes). Then, their first child was born and everything changed. The couple said, "Life became a constant battle." They struggled not to let the fast pace of their lives totally consume them. They could see their family life beginning to blossom and felt it was more important than business or sports. They scribbled four priorities on Post-it Notes: God, family, exercise, and work, in that order. After recording how they spent their time for a week, the couple discovered a disturbing trend. They spent most of their time at work and at the gym. They spent a little bit of time together as a family each evening. And they only thought about God one hour each Sunday when they were at church. Based on how they were spending their time, their priorities were upside down!

Douglas Steere, the Quaker teacher and writer, tells the story of an explorer traveling in Africa, accompanied by a group of native carriers. On a particular morning many days into the journey, the carriers refused to continue. When asked why, they replied that they had to wait for their souls to catch up.[4]

Years ago we drove across the Hudson River to New York to experience the Broadway play, *Stop the World, I Want to Get Off.* The pace of the play was fast and sobering. The pace of life for most of us is breathtaking. I asked a busy friend how he had space for any focused time with God. He said, "I get it on the run."

Not only are we on the run—we are in constant contact with work, family, and friends. We drive with a phone to our ear because we must stay in touch every possible moment, even if it kills us, despite the police telling us strongly, "Stop your car before making a call."

A former professor of mine, Dr. Wayne Oates, used to tell us, "If you do not take your Sabbaths when they come, you will take them all at once."[5] One Chinese dialect uses two characters to represent busyness. One is heart. The other is kill. Busyness = heart kill.

The Need to Take Time Out

At Laity Lodge we often heard guests say, "I didn't realize how tired I was." "I can't believe it. I slept four hours this afternoon." We are a tired nation. Many of us carry heart loads that need to be lightened—a recent death of a loved one, a divorce, estrangement from family members, financial difficulties, the loss of a job, a move, the uncertainty of retirement, depression, health problems, guilt from sin. Men and women need a safe place where they can share these burdens and see them in the light of the action of God on our behalf—forgiveness, grace, love, and presence. A retreat can create such an environment.

A retreat often helps guests find a new consciousness of God. It transforms their lives and gives them new eyes to see that their daily work serves God. Family relations become more honest, open, and loving. Service to others becomes a higher priority in the use of time, money, and attention in prayer.

Retreats provide a time set aside from our normal pursuits. A special time dedicated for the purpose of physical, emotional, and spiritual renewal. Time for important questions to surface: Who am I? Where have I been? Where am I? And where am I going? When we open ourselves to silence, God awakens us to his Spirit who is always alive and active in us and in the world.

In his classic book *Renewal in Retreats,* John Casteel says we come face to face with our compulsions and habitual behavior when we detach ourselves from daily life. For example, an incessant talker balks at the possibility of hours of silence. The detachment of a retreat invites introspection. And introspection cuts through our self-images and egocentricity, forcing us to come to terms with our own selfish patterns of life and helping us better love and serve God and our neighbors.[6]

We only get one life on earth, and something deep inside the heart desires a life of meaning. Some call it a God-shaped void. Viktor Frankl found in his Nazi prison experience that men and women survived if they had a solid reason for living. Perhaps the destruction of the Trade Towers and part of the Pentagon were calls for all of us to wake up to life—to God.[7]

Carole, my wife, and I visited a longtime friend of her family. The friend had supper ready every working day when her husband came home. Their meals were seldom interrupted by conversation. Each evening her husband ate, read the evening paper and several financial journals, and went to sleep. She worried about his bulk and his recent severe heart attack. "I am waiting for him to die," she said. "You know you can't live on sandwiches made out of money."

Men and women need opportunities to confront life, to explore the large questions, and to run into God. More than three and a half million people a year attend retreats. In the past fifty years we have seen a surge of interest in setting some time aside to seek heart peace and meaning. One place striving to meet these needs is a unique Christian retreat center nestled by a spring-fed river in the Texas Hill Country. Its name is Laity Lodge.

Notes

1 Thomas à Kempis, *The Imitation of Christ.*

2 William Blake, "The Little Black Boy," *Songs of Innocence.*

3 This conversation so moved me that I wrote a poem expressing the man's feelings (see Appendix A).

4 Douglas Steere. *Time to Spare* (New York: Harper and Brothers, 1949) 87.

5 Wayne Oates made similar comments in his book *Your Right to Rest* (Philadelphia: Westminster Press, 1984).

6 John Casteel. *Renewal in Retreats* (New York: Association Press, 1959) 20-21.

7 In my poem, "Breaking Down Fences," I have described the process of finding real life (see Appendix A).

Chapter 2

Wellsprings of the Dream: The Butt Family Story

Family Background

The story of Laity Lodge began with two families, the Butts and the Holdsworths, in Tennessee and England. At the beginning of the twentieth century, Charles Clarence and Florence Butt moved from the Volunteer State to the Texas Hill Country. They had heard that the Lone Star State—with its clean air, dry climate, and gentle winters—was ideal for family members with tuberculosis. They chose Kerrville, a town on the banks of the Guadalupe River, sixty-five miles west of San Antonio and ninety miles southwest of Austin.

Howard E. Butt Sr.'s father, Charles C. Butt, never did get well. To survive, Florence Butt started a grocery store on the first floor of their home in Kerrville. While cleaning out the downstairs, she found a copy of the New Testament. It seemed a good omen, so she knelt and prayed. Her faith was basic to her life, and this discovery was a clear affirmation.

The youngest son, Howard Edward, was the delivery boy. He filled his little red wagon with groceries and walked down the street in high-top laced shoes and knee-pants, delivering the items to their many pay-by-the-month customers. This boy, with his fine mind and his early budding business genius, grew up to develop one of the largest privately owned grocery chains in America—the H. E. Butt Grocery Company.

In the late nineteenth century, Thomas Kirk Holdsworth lived in Ripponden, northern England. He was an educator at a school named Making Place Hall, near the Scottish border. Due to the decline of the wool trading business, the school's enrollment dropped, and it finally closed. He decided to move his family to Texas. It was 1880.

Under some of the land purchase arrangements then available through the young state government, Mr. Holdsworth purchased a tract of land in Texas. He brought his family by ship to New York. From there, they traveled by train to Uvalde, Texas, on to Pearsall, and then to the little town of Derby. At Derby, they disembarked and went by foot, horse, and carriage to the land he had bought, located between Derby and Crystal City in Zavala County. It is hard to imagine a schoolmaster from England living in that country in 1880. To this day, the area still has no major roads. The dusty, scrub country takes eighteen to twenty acres to support one cow. Even goats have a difficult time. The heat often soars higher than one hundred degrees. For the first three years, the Holdsworth family lived in tents that held in the stifling heat of summer and failed to keep out the cold wind from the north during the brief winters.

Mr. Holdsworth eked out a living as a rancher and teacher. According to later generations, he was so poor that he traveled around Texas and sold sewing machines for extra money to keep body and soul together. Perhaps he sold those sewing machines just to get off the ranch!

During these travels, Mr. Holdsworth sold a machine to a family living at the present Laity Lodge location in the Frio Canyon. Later he sent his oldest son, Thomas, from Zavala County up to the Frio Canyon in Real County to collect for it. The trade agreement had been a flock of sheep for the machine. So in 1882, Thomas, at age sixteen, embarked on an arduous seventy-mile trip on a little rattail pony, up through Uvalde into the Frio Canyon. He had to spend the night with the people who purchased the machine. With his sharp British accent, he told them about the trip across the Atlantic Ocean on the ship. His stories dazzled the family, and their young son uttered this priceless line: "I ain't never seen no ship. I wish't I could see one comin' up the Frio."

A special daughter of that young Thomas Holdsworth—Mary—would become a college graduate, a teacher, and the wife of Howard E. Butt, Sr., the founder of the H. E. Butt Grocery Company.

A Marriage of Minds and Souls

On July 10, 1924, just after having become engaged, Mr. Butt wrote a letter to his fiancée, Mary Holdsworth. She was a student at the University of Texas in Austin when she read this letter about the marriage they envisioned:

> We have no right to live to ourselves alone . . . we cannot evade our duty to God and our fellow man. And it is a mistake, even from a selfish viewpoint, to try to do so. For we make ourselves grow smaller, and our happiness is more limited by so doing. Love crowned, yes, that is the first essential; dedicated to service—may God grant that our united life may be felt as a great and lasting good in our community; broad minded—I'm sure that we will both be that; we must have only the highest and best thoughts—any other foundation would not support the edifice we dream of building. May God give me strength to so live as to always deserve your faith, and may He help me build my character to what you want it to be. And you are right, dear, about the necessity for courtesy—and individuality also.[1]

On April 9, 1935, Mr. Butt turned forty and wrote the following:

> As I pause to take stock of myself on this milestone of life, to take pride in the things accomplished and to visualize the possibilities ahead, I resolve not to be content to rest on the mediocre success I have accomplished but to concentrate my energy and plans on the larger possibilities ahead—to read and study worthwhile things, to prepare myself for a larger place—to make myself more thoroughly familiar with my business and the entire food industry with this larger place in view, to contact big men in this and other industries to help me to grow. To work out the few things in our setup that constitute a source of worry to me, at all times keeping my affairs in the best of shape for any eventuality.
>
> To not lose sight of my duty to God and my fellow man, enlarging constantly as my position warrants on our charitable and community work, taking care to develop this side above all others. To so live that my boy may hear of my record and dealings with

pride. To mold and train him to have the fine big character he is capable of developing.

To develop my own character and personality—not permitting trivial things to deflect my course from my larger ambition. To care better for my health each day, maintaining myself at the highest possible point of fitness physical and mental.

To have a closer relation and a better understanding of the problems of my employees and associates.

Resolve that the next decade shall mark greater accomplishments than this decade just closed, with God's help.

Three children were born to Howard and Mary: Howard Jr., Eleanor, and Charles.

The H. E. Butt Foundation

In 1933 Mr. and Mrs. Butt created a nonprofit foundation. Its limited funds would help meet the needs of families, children, and the community.

In 1954 they purchased the 1,900-acre Wolfe Ranch near Leakey, Texas. They intended to make it possible for children to have an experience on a ranch at no cost. As a boy, Mr. Butt had loved visiting ranches but seldom had the opportunity. His dream for the 1,900 acres grew from those childhood experiences into a mature vision: "If I can ever afford it, I want to provide an opportunity for people, especially children, to have time on a ranch." Fifty years later, the H. E. Butt family has developed its property on the east fork of the Frio River into five camps plus Laity Lodge. The canyon now has a total capacity of 700. More than 25,000 people from 380 groups came to the Frio Canyon for two or more days in 2005. All five camps are free. Guests bring their own bedding, food, and programs. The foundation provides excellent facilities, including fully equipped kitchens, dining rooms, well-kept dorms, a waterfront for swimming and fishing, and space for play. Three of the camps have tennis courts. The civic and faith-minded couple bought the ranch and then gave it away.

In diary entries during the early camp period, Mrs. Butt wrote, "I hope as many as 100 children, and some adults, will experience God and the beauty of this place, as we have found it." At the time, she and her husband never imagined more than 25,000 people would use the facilities each year.

The Vision of Howard Butt, Jr.

Mr. Butt's oldest son, Howard Jr., began stacking groceries while in grade school. He learned all aspects of the business. He often traveled with his father to new store openings, and he was always amazed at his father's energy. His father took stairs two at a time and could spot, on the fly, weaknesses and strengths in a store.

While young Howard was being groomed to lead the grocery company, he also was leading youth revivals and citywide religious meetings. He spoke in churches, auditoriums, and football stadiums. His contagious passion for God awakened thousands of teens, college students, and adults to the transforming power of Jesus Christ.

Speaking extensively and working full-time as a vice president in the grocery business meant a tight schedule. Weekends often took Howard Jr. to far-flung revival meetings. On more than one occasion, Howard flew home from a meeting in the pre-dawn hours on Monday. His wife, Barbara Dan, would meet him at the airport carrying a clean shirt and then drive him directly to the grocery company office.

But eventually, burning the candle at both ends became too much, and Howard began suffering from severe clinical depression. To be a Baptist lay evangelist who needed psychiatric help was surely the worst possible scenario, he thought. Then he discovered the remarkable gifts that came wrapped inside his depression. He began learning about the powerful emotions within up-close personal and familial relationships.

He also felt drawn to Trinitarian servant-leadership, spiritual discernment, nurturing, administration, writing, preaching, and planning events with the right mix between leaders and participants. He increasingly focused his work into a prophetic word about the calling of *all* God's people in *all* their lives and work, to lead a prophetic organization to embody Christian authenticity and unity in teams, and to call the church as a whole to deeper levels of discipleship and renewal. He gave more and more attention to the ministries that were developing in the Frio Canyon.

Tolstoy wrote, "The only significance of life consists in helping to establish the kingdom of God; and this can be done only by means of the acknowledgment and profession of the truth by each one of us."[2] In light of Tolstoy's words, Howard Butt Jr. lives a strategically significant life. Howard heard God's call. He has received a specific truth to profess, and he has spent his life establishing the kingdom of God in the Frio Canyon. He continued his family's vision, manifesting God's love by serving others. But he also acknowledged his own unique vision to minister to the laity. He said, "We're prone to see the work of the church as only tied to the gathered, institutional church. But the scattered church—the laity out in the world—that's New Testament Christianity. That's where the really tough work of the church takes place."

I was one of many affected by his ministry. I responded to the call of God to a church-centered vocation at a Baylor pre-school retreat at which Howard spoke. The youth revival movement of the '40s and '50s had its beginning at Baylor University, and Howard Butt was the general chairman of the explosive 1946 Waco meeting. Howard was invited to be a speaker at one of the early prayer breakfasts of President Eisenhower. He was named by President Kennedy to the first committee on Equal Employment Opportunity.

Others have been touched by his life through the Layman's Leadership Institutes in which he teamed with Billy Graham. These three-day meetings encouraged business professionals to follow Christ in their homes, businesses, churches, and communities. Still others were transformed through the North American Congress of the Laity where President Ford served as honorary chairman. Business leaders from America and other countries continue to be challenged through the Laity Lodge Leadership Forums held every other year. Under Howard's guidance, nearly 1,500 children a year learn about Christ through the Laity Lodge Youth Camp. Still others have been changed by God through Howard's expansion of his parents' original free camp vision.

Howard Butt is from a servant family. He serves as vice chairman of the H. E. Butt Grocery Company and president of the H. E. Butt Foundation. His sister, Eleanor, serves on the board of the grocery company and a variety of organizations, particularly Bread for the World. Charles, his brother, serves as chairman and chief executive of the H. E. Butt Grocery Company, which has expanded greatly under his leadership, always with his high view of serving its communities.

Howard serves the community of south Texas by offering them spiritual renewal. He is a bridge builder: between denominations, between laity and clergy, between the "secular" and the "spiritual," between religion and the social sciences, between work and family, and between the church and the world. Howard lives his life by this vision. He serves Jesus through this vision. And with God's grace, this vision will continue to ripple through heaven and earth.

Laity Lodge

During the past forty-plus years, Howard has given his primary attention to Laity Lodge and the various ministries of the H. E. Butt Foundation. As an encouragement to Howard Jr., his parents created a place where he could focus his ministry. After exploring retreat centers in Europe and the United States, he built Laity Lodge. Thus, one of the six camps located on the 1,900 acres became a Christian retreat center that serves adults throughout the year.

Laity Lodge has grown a great deal from the original layout that consisted of a motel-style guest lodge, the Great Hall meeting room, the dining room, a tiny office, and an apartment for the Butts. The foundation has built many other facilities, including a small satellite of Laity Lodge called the Quiet House. My predecessor, Bill Cody, dreamed of a simple place of quiet solitude, a cottage for silence, meditation, and prayer. With Mary Holdsworth Butt, he planned the exquisite, tiny house of prayer for one person or a married couple. The money for the cottage came from donations from interested people outside the Butt family, the first building in the canyon financed in that way.

Laity Lodge also includes an amphitheater and a complex of buildings dedicated to the arts, named after members of the Cody family. The most recent Laity Lodge facility is the Hovde House, a beautiful double apartment for Laity Lodge directors, speakers, musicians, artists, and writers-in-residence.

These ministries did not begin with money, power, and prestige but with illness, poverty, and depression. Such struggles allowed for the creative power of the Spirit of God. In 2 Corinthians 12:9-10, the Apostle Paul writes God's response to his request to have a thorn removed from his life: "'My grace is all you need; for my power is strongest when you are weak.' I am most happy, then, to be proud of any weaknesses, in order to feel the protection of Christ's power over me. I am content with weaknesses, insults, hardships, persecutions, and difficulties for Christ's sake. For when I am weak, then I am strong."[3] If God can take illness, poverty, and depression and create a place like Laity Lodge, then there is hope for all of us.

Notes

1 All quotes from the H. E. Butt Foundation are used with permission.

2 Tolstoy, Count Leo, *The Kingdom of God within You*, ch. 12.

3 Good News Bible, Collins World, 1997, published by the United Bible Societies.

Chapter 3

God's Timing for the Dream: The Founding Director

A Moment in Time

The founding director of Laity Lodge, J. Keith Miller,[1] describes the confluence of cultural and personal forces coming together in God's perfect timing to make a place like Laity Lodge possible. The Laity Lodge program began in the wave of creative energy that flowed across America, generated by the victory of the U.S. and its allies at the end of the Second World War. The first visible, measurable expression of this new energy in the institutional church was the construction of new buildings. Thousands of yards of concrete were poured into new churches and their parking lots across America.

But problems arose when it came to educating the masses of "new people." During the war, many had prayed intimately to God in foxholes. Others at home prayed equally as intimately for their soldiers and sailors in battle.

One difficulty at that time in the 1950s was that most adult Christian education programs were cognitive study courses. They didn't deal with the reality of the fear and intensity people had experienced while praying about survival for themselves or their loved ones. Instead, in many church adult classes, people learned historical biblical information *about* God and faith based on doctrinally sound concepts. But survivors from the war wanted more experiential knowledge—even though in many cases they didn't know how to ask for what they wanted. Something was missing.

In church adult classes or Bible study groups, people were reluctant to talk about such private subjects as one's own doubt, fear, failure, and loss. It was equally difficult for church members to talk about their personal faith or to integrate their faith into their business or personal lives in practical, natural ways. And the cognitive principles they learned in church classes didn't seem to have anything to do with the highly charged experiences they had had in the war. The cognitive information just didn't seem real.

The desire to "be real" was a national issue in both secular and religious institutions. People were like little chicks, trapped in their shells of emotional isolation and unable to be honest about their feelings and needs. Some repressed their unacceptable fears and failures and denied they had problems. Others turned to compulsive work—even church work—to bury their unacceptable feelings. The "human potential movement" unfolded as psychologists began to develop small group methods to help people break out of their cognitive prisons and find ways to overcome their fear of intimacy and their denial. Three different approaches to "freedom" emerged.

One approach used various kinds of direct *confrontation.* Participants were directly challenged about anything they did or said that the group or its leaders felt was not authentic. Some participants did learn to live with more emotional freedom; but for others, the direct confrontation experience was frightening and painful. It was a little like trying to help chicks hatch by smashing the shells. Although there was remarkable success (e.g., T-Groups and William Glassers' "Reality Therapy" Groups), some people came away from such experiences psychologically or emotionally bruised.

A second approach freed people to be authentic through voluntary *personal sharing.*[1] In this technique, the leader or therapist listened attentively. For example, Carl Rogers, a psychologist, listened to people and reflected calmly and nonjudgmentally exactly what he heard his clients saying. Many felt heard and understood, often for the first time in their lives, and were drawn out of their shells into emotional freedom to relate more intimately. Very few felt bruised by this approach, but it was not direct or solution-oriented enough for many.

A third approach encouraged people to try new levels of *personal risk*—risks that varied from verbal sharing of their own faults and sins to physical/social risks like ropes courses or survival programs. Many people found new personal freedom through these methods. Others, however, had unexpected negative aftereffects, including guilt, shame, and broken relationships.

The church's responses to the call for reality and personal relevance were more traditional and cognitive. Church leaders formed educational task groups and classes to deal with members' complaints that the church was not relevant to the issues of contemporary life. But only a few church leaders seemed to perceive the problem as pertaining to the emotional pain and spiritual thirst of internally imprisoned souls. Many of these Christians were in the midst of loving families and churches but were restless, bored, or unhappy in their relationships. Respected church members were living in pious denial, unaware that it might be appropriate, even good and helpful, to deal with these personal issues openly in order to become the loving people Jesus described as being God's children. In fact, many ministers and lay teachers thought being personal about one's problems and sins in Christian contexts was *not* appropriate. Such people thought healthy Christians did not share their sins with each other, in spite of the clear instructions of the author of James 5:16: "Make this your common practice: Confess your sins to *each other* and pray for each other so that you can live together whole and healed" (*The Message*).

Many Christian ministers did preach the grace and love of God through Christ. But they didn't tell people exactly *how* they were supposed to *express* this same grace and love to their families and associates in their secular vocations. From the outside, long-term church members appeared to be every bit as limited in their personal relation to God and neighbors as any other business and professional people.

The church needed a new approach, one that would help free those imprisoned. Too many Christians were afraid to be known intimately by their families, colleagues, and fellow Christians.

Finding the First Director

Keith Miller was in the oil exploration business in Oklahoma, trying to live out these principles in his own personal and business relationships. He spoke to seminar groups, discovering what Christian people thought *really* blocked them from relating to God or others. He began by handing out 3- by 5-inch cards and asking people to respond anonymously to the question: "What is it that blocks you from being the free and loving person you believe God wants you to be?" Participants' answers revealed doubts about some Christian doctrines, the fear of looking foolish, a broken marriage, an unhappy relationship with a child, a sexual frustration, or compulsion or affair, a drinking problem, financial insecurity, and many other recurring fears or doubts. These led to anxiety or other behavioral symptoms like insomnia, loss of hope, or increased fear of sharing their own reality with other Christians. Within a few years, he collected hundreds of responses to this question.

Keith said, "These issues were not dealt with in most sermons I heard or adult education classes I attended. And yet these were the very private problems many people believed were keeping them from experiencing and sharing the love of God that Jesus brought." In further research, he noticed that Jesus' teaching to the people about God's new kingdom and reign was almost totally related to the problems and personal issues of the people to whom he was bringing the message (e.g., stories and parables in Matthew, Mark, and Luke).

He soon realized it was more effective to deal haltingly with real and specific problems than to speak beautifully about theological issues. "Speaking vulnerably about my own experiences concerning the anonymous issues laypeople had written on the cards was very instructive for me." Keith spoke honestly about his own fears and failures and pointed to God as the only hope he had found of getting the courage to face these painful things. And an incredible thing began to happen. "Individuals *voluntarily began to share their own failures,* and a real sense of hope and expectation developed in the room. People became enthusiastic about learning, and they reported feeling safer."

Keith began to dream about finding a place to be with laypeople for a weekend and share what he was learning about integrating faith and love into everyday living.

Within a month he received an invitation to speak from a businessman he didn't know, a man who was to become one of his dearest friends and Christian brothers—a grocery chain executive from South Texas named Howard E. Butt Jr. "He invited me, and a number of other men, to speak at a 'Layman's Leadership Institute,' a meeting of business and professional men and women from the U.S. and Canada, in Louisville, Kentucky. I accepted his invitation."

Several months later, Keith and his wife met Howard and Barbara Dan over lunch. During that meal, they talked about their lives. Howard asked him what he saw in the Christian renewal movement beginning to spread into most of the major denominations. Keith told Howard about his faith discoveries.

Howard looked thoughtful, and then he asked, "What do you plan to do, Keith?" Keith told him that he was recently thinking about finding some sort of a conference center near Oklahoma City. He wanted to teach business and professional people and their families what he was discovering about communication and Christianity. Howard looked surprised.

Keith knew little about Howard and what he did—except that he was a successful businessman who sponsored large seminars about Christianity. They had never had a private conversation. Then Howard told Keith that he and his family were in the process of building a conference center for laypeople in the Texas Hill Country.

Some months later, Howard asked Keith to tell his story at the opening of that center in June 1961. Dr. Elton Trueblood was the primary speaker. The title of Dr. Trueblood's new book, *Your Other Vocation,* was the subject for the weekend. After the conference, Keith's family moved to Richmond, Indiana, where he studied with Elton Trueblood in the new Earlham School of Religion, a Quaker theological school.

A year later, Howard invited Keith to move to Leakey, Texas, where Keith became the first director of Laity Lodge.

Notes

1 Keith Miller wrote the material in chapters 3 and 4. It has been edited to fit the format of this book.

2 See Carl Rogers, *Client-Centered Therapy* (Boston: Houghton Mifflin, 1951), and Paul Tournier, *The Meaning of Persons* (New York: Harper and Row, 1957).

Chapter 4

Scaffolding for the Dream: The Early Years with Keith Miller

A Unique Approach

Unlike Howard, who sponsored big conferences, Keith's focus had always been on working with small groups. Together, Howard and Keith hammered out a model for a weekend conference for laypeople who might be serious about living out their Christianity in their vocations. Their theological backgrounds were very different. Howard was a Southern Baptist, and Keith belonged to the Episcopal Church. Howard's theological training at Southwestern Baptist Theological Seminary had been conservative, strongly biblical with a doctrinal emphasis. Howard was an accomplished evangelistic preacher who had spoken all over the world with Billy Graham. His experience and reputation as a prominent preacher and evangelist was international. Keith's theological training at Berkeley Divinity School in New Haven, Connecticut (Episcopal), was also biblical, but with a more literary/critical emphasis. Keith was steeped in the lives of the saints and their spiritual direction for living, and in "relational theology"— understanding and expressing one's Christian faith in terms of relationships more than doctrinal formulae. Keith's experience consisted mostly of speaking to adult Sunday school classes and small groups in homes.

Most Christian conference centers at that time focused on traditional Bible teaching, "social action" through changing political and social structures, or the behavioral components of emotional and psychological relationships. Howard and Keith came up with an approach to a weekend conference that was unique at the time. Deeply committed to God in Jesus Christ, to loving people, and to the primacy of the Bible, they decided to include *both* a biblical teacher *and* a counselor-relational person on the team at every conference. Their own input at the conferences dealt with the personal, theological, and relational aspects of God's saving message in the New Testament. From their own experiences of dealing with emotional blocks to commitment and change that kept them from fulfilling Jesus' command to love God and other people, they illustrated what they taught. Unwittingly, Howard and Keith created a synergistic program that emphasized healthy biblical teaching *and* informal personal direction. Both elements led people toward emotional and spiritual maturity. They could then return to their own worlds to love and minister to hurting, isolated people bypassed by traditional approaches to "outreach."

Howard and Keith believed that many adult members of churches—including themselves—were still afraid to own and express who they really were, even to those close to them. But they also believed that the antidote to fear is love (1 John 4), and they believed in sharing their real lives with each other (Jas 5). Keith said, "We believed that if we really concentrated on being honest about our reality and faith, on listening to and loving every person who came to the conferences, God could create an atmosphere of safety and warmth." He continued, "We and other imprisoned 'chicks' might feel safe enough to peck our way out of our shells from the inside—each at his or her own speed."

To create an atmosphere where this could happen, they treated Laity Lodge as if it were their "summer place" to which they invited the participants to come for a weekend visit. Keith provided a list of some of the things they did to express love to the people who came to the conferences:

1. Before each group arrived, we studied the list of participants and tried to learn their names. Then we prayed specifically for each participant.

2. We discussed any information we had about their families and vocations that might help us know them better.
3. We met the people when they arrived on Friday and helped them carry their luggage to their rooms. Our wives served tea in the evening after the first meeting.
4. We encouraged the kitchen and housekeeping staffs and groundskeepers to do excellent work and to be friendly and helpful to the participants.

Training a Team of Witnesses

Almost from the beginning, Howard and Keith felt that one of their primary goals was training laypeople to train other people to do what they were doing (2 Tim 2:2). Within a few weeks, they began to invite participants to come back and work with them as part of the leadership team. They chose those whose lives had been changed, inviting them to speak to the group about what had happened to them since their first conference at Laity—the good and the bad things—as they had tried to live for Christ.

These witnesses turned out to be one of the most exciting parts of each meeting. The awakened Christians hadn't been at it long enough to know a lot of pious Christian language. Consequently, they just told it as it was: their successes and their failures, as they tried to love people in their families and vocations for Christ's sake. Instead of announcing they had been victorious, some said it had not been easy, but they now had hope that they could change. Some reported less anxiety and more closeness with family members and God. Older Christians were stunned—and then delighted—to see God's footprints in these people's lives.

These witnesses met with the professional speakers before each session. Howard and Keith wanted to show these sharp, young laypeople—many were new Christians—how other Christian speakers and writers handled their own anxiety, etc. Witnesses found outstanding mentors, and some speakers were surprised to find friendships that lasted for years. People from both groups found inspiration and rejuvenation. Some of the witnesses were invited back as small-group leaders. Keith said, "It's not possible for me to convey the sense of wonder we felt as Howard and I watched all this unfold."

A Panel of Questions

At most conferences, Howard and Keith included one session in which every speaker sat on a panel to address anonymous questions from the participants. Keith said, "It was a little unnerving for some of the speakers to abandon their prepared material to deal with these questions. That flexibility was unique in most of the speakers' experiences—especially since the questions often dealt with issues that were very personal and even intimate." He added, "In most cases, the speakers responded personally with profound honesty and wisdom, providing motivation for us all. The people attending were amazed to see outstanding communicators addressing their real, personal blocks to loving God and people."

The Role of Silence

On Sunday mornings, Howard and Keith set aside a time of silence. Guests could make a specific silent decision to take the hypothesis that God is real. They could silently commit themselves to living with Christ as the dominant focus of their lives—if not forever, then at least for a month, just to see what would happen. Why a silent decision? The anonymous questions revealed that many Christians had been shamed as children (or as adults) by overzealous Christian evangelists, Sunday school teachers, or other new Christians. They felt manipulated by those trying to push them into making a commitment to Christ through fear or peer pressure. Giving people permission and a time and place to take a private step toward God turned out to be a significant experience for many people. Many mainline churchgoers had never had a specific opportunity to make such a new beginning.

After these sessions, Howard and Keith advised those who made silent commitments that they could tell their leaders. The leaders supported them in finding direction and providing guidance for their new adventure. Howard and Keith recommended biblical reference books, devotional disciplines, and other resources for a serious Christian journey. Much of the classic spiritual guidance at that time came from European Catholics and was several hundred years old. So Keith wrote a small book, *The Taste of New Wine,* primarily a compilation of presentations he had made at earlier Laity Lodge conferences. These talks were about beginning to live a life committed to living for God and loving God and people.

Dealing with a Short Shelf Life

Howard and Keith soon realized that a weekend experience had a "short shelf life"—unless some significant reinforcement came within a few days. So, on the final morning, Howard and Keith suggested books to read and gave the conference participants suggestions and handouts about ways to begin praying and reading the Bible each day. Keith related, "At first we were stumped about how to deal with the lack of continuity the participants discovered in their local church programs when they got home. That's how we moved into providing spiritual direction through personal correspondence and the telephone."

Finally, they remembered how Paul, Barnabas, and others had spread the gospel message in the first century by using the time-intensive method of starting small groups of new believers around the Roman world and then continuing to communicate with, teach, and visit the groups. So Howard and Keith offered to meet with groups back in their own cities one weeknight a week for eight weeks, following the conferences. They required all the participants in any such proposed follow-up groups to agree ahead of time to attend all eight of the meetings to which Howard and Keith came (excepting emergencies). This was when things really began to happen. The people in those groups kept coming back to Laity Lodge and bringing new people with them. Some of those first participants have continued to return for more than forty years.

Keith said, "Looking back, our commitment to those people would no doubt be considered by most standards a little insane. We were driving up to 250 miles one way each week to some of the meetings, and we were not charging them any fees. There was no question in the participants' minds that we were serious about the new life of living Christ's adventure."

Keith burned out after a couple of years. The conferences eventually got too large in number to continue those eight-week follow-up visits (although every director since has done some form of follow-up with individuals). "But Howard and I were young, full of vinegar, and we felt it was going to take something like this kind of hospitality and continued loving attention to show people that Jesus is alive. And he is a serious people-lover too."

Keith and Howard prayed that they might create a new kind of loving center where serious Christian adventurers could learn to receive and give God's kind of love in a tough and sometimes uncaring secular world. "We tried in the only ways we could think of to support and encourage the members of the follow-up groups as they took their faith into the secular worlds of their own hometowns."

Talent Scouts for God

As Howard and Keith saw people come out of their shells and express the love and life they were discovering in creative ways, they began to feel strongly that God, through Laity Lodge, was not about recruiting religious marines. Keith said, "If we are made in God's creative image, then when God frees us from the bonds of our fear-filled eggshells, our primary task is not to become 'super religious.'" Laity Lodge tries to help people on Christ's adventure to discover and develop the creative gifts and aptitudes that God has already put in them. From the beginning, Howard and Keith encouraged Laity Lodge graduates to write books, create beautiful paintings, sculpture, and music, and to develop creative ministries to serve neglected groups. To their delight, participants from the first days made strong statements of beauty in sculptures and paintings, some of which are still at the lodge. Others have made significant contributions to positive changes in our culture through creative political and social involvement. Others have written books, poetry, and music. Still others are using their gifts in the business, professional, and religious worlds.

Keith left Laity Lodge as director in fall 1965, after four summers of conferences that helped Howard get the program off the ground. Each director since has added essential pieces to the educational and spiritual dimensions of today's Laity Lodge.

Chapter 5

Unfolding of the Dream: The Bill Cody Era

The Friendship of Howard Butt and Bill Cody

Betty Anne Cody recounted the story of her husband's time as director of Laity Lodge.[1] In their Baylor University and Southwestern Seminary days, 1944 to 1949, Howard Butt and Bill Cody become good friends. In college, they prayed, planned, and preached as part of the youth revival movement. The bonds of service and dedication to God grew strong and enduring. Through the 1950s, they kept in touch, meeting at Ridgecrest, North Carolina, and other places, catching up on each other's lives and callings. Howard fulfilled his calls to business and to ministry involving lay leadership. Bill moved from the seminary to work as pastor to students at the University of Kentucky, then to serve with the Baptist Sunday School Board in Nashville, working with college students across the nation. Following this period, Bill was in the personnel division of the Foreign Mission Board for nine years.

Both men were gifted in working with people, in communication, and in connecting with crowds and with individuals. Their skills and histories came together in fall of 1963, when Bill worked as Howard's personal assistant and as director of the Layman's Leadership Institutes. Combined with other duties, this work used Bill's abilities in planning, in organizing, and in working skillfully with people.

Layman's Leadership Institutes, Howard's annual gatherings of national business executives, soon expanded to three times a year. Set in beautiful resort hotels, these meetings gave encouragement to businesspeople and their spouses and enabled them to live out the teachings of Jesus in their workplaces much more completely. The programs included witnesses who told their own stories, thus encouraging the listeners and letting them know they were not alone in trying to apply their faith to their work. Bill organized these powerful meetings with remarkable effectiveness.

For years, Howard had been searching for the right additional vehicle to further his vision of spiritual awakening in the churches through laypeople, and thus out into the broader world. He had traveled widely, refining ideas—from Germany's post-World War II Lay Academies with their mighty *Kirchentag* rallies, to Scotland, learning more of George MacLeod's Iona Community, to California and Henrietta Mears' Forest Home Christian Conference Center with its charming Lakeview Lodge. Even Jamaica's Frenchman's Cove Resort helped him visualize a setting.

After years of prayer and consultation, his mother determined to "build a tool for Howard's hands." At last, Howard's vision would become reality.

Laity Lodge had its first retreat in June 1961. Betty Anne said, "Howard met Keith Miller and called this exceptional layman to work with him at Laity Lodge in the summer of 1962. Though we are now familiar with the combination of study, witness, and small groups, at that time this was extremely innovative programming." The small-group movement was growing.[2] Keith and Howard took the risk of trying new ideas that enabled them to lead the most effective retreats possible. This principle became basic to Laity Lodge programming.

The Transition

In spring of 1965, Keith decided to enter graduate school at the University of Texas. Howard knew Laity Lodge had a great future and wanted to bring a leader of established experience in directing retreats and conferences. He asked Bill Cody to be interim director during the national search. Bill had already been drawn to Laity Lodge and to the retreat setting. He moved his family to San Antonio and worked with Keith that summer, taking full leadership as interim director in October 1965. Betty Anne said, "In later years recalling that transition, Bill said he was never so scared as he was in trying to follow

Keith's leadership. That anxiety gave him the edge to put his own personality into the retreats, sparking continued growth for Laity Lodge."

Bill continued his work with Layman's Leadership Institutes and his other duties with Howard's ministries. And he agreed to lead Laity Lodge until Howard could find the person he believed was God's man for the place. Bill directed the retreats through 1966. In 1967, while still the interim director, he began the first summer Institute of Lay Studies. In contrast to the weekend retreats that focused on specific church congregations, these guests stayed for a week in the summer. The extended institutes became popular. That same year, in summer of 1967, the Laity Lodge Youth Camps opened with James (Frog) Sullivan leading the camps under Bill's leadership. In 1968, Bill became the official director of Laity Lodge. At the invitation of Mrs. Butt Sr., he also became an administrator of H. E. Butt Foundation Camps.

Growth and Development

The Laity Lodge retreats continued to grow, serving churches of many denominations. Men and women came from all parts of south and west Texas. They came from other cities and states to attend weeklong conferences. Howard opened Laity Lodge to various denominations, and a remarkable phenomenon began in the Christian communities of southwest Texas. Many different church groups came together at Laity Lodge. They heard Bible teachers from several denominations teaching the same truth. They heard witnesses from a different part of God's family sharing how God was present in all of life's struggles and joys. They learned that God's people were more alike than different. Pastors of different denominations came to respect each other, and many met in their home cities, building on the groups they had experienced at Laity Lodge. Christians gained new courage to put the teachings of Jesus into their work and play. They learned how to apply Jesus' words to their relationships. Relational theology moved from their heads to their hearts and into their behaviors.

Many trusted Christ for the first time. When guests returned home, other people noticed the change. Other churches wanted to share in the experiences God offered at Laity Lodge. More churches reserved weekends for their members, and many put their names on waiting lists. Soon almost every weekend was booked.

When choosing speakers and teachers for retreats, Bill sought out the exciting young leaders of those days. Some of them were writing books on the relational teachings of Christ and how his words applied to relationships in the family and the community. These ideas were a key emphasis of the programming. The "young lions" of denominations came once and wanted to come again. They brought their wives and children to the canyon, and all received the ministries of grace. Sometimes teachers came for an extra week. Laity paid the airfare of the spouses as a ministry to each speaker's marriage. The effect of this ministry behind the scenes was quiet and deep. Bill always heard the speakers and got to know them in advance. He wanted to be sure they would be effective in the setting of the lodge. Speakers who could motivate and inspire crowds of thousands might not fit into the intimacy of retreats with fifty to eighty people. Bill and Howard chose the leaders carefully. Howard had many connections and brought nationally known speakers. Bill brought lesser known speakers to teach alongside popular speakers. Once people heard the new speaker, they planned to come again when he was the main speaker.

Bill's Gifts as Director

From the early days, the innovative planning of Howard, Keith, and Bill combined strong Bible study with the insights of psychology. Often, a seminary Bible professor would be on the program with a Christian psychiatrist. They coordinated their subject matter and applied it through the questions given for the small-group discussions. This method proved to be a powerful way for people to integrate what they learned.

Bill believed strongly in laughter and play as part of the retreat experience. The Frio River always provided guests with a place to meet, swim, sun, and talk. The tennis court was loud with laughter of beginners and skilled players. Everyone had a great time playing together. Hikers could take to the hills and feel they were in uncharted territory. Others needed rest. They could sleep the deep sleep that renewed their bodies from their busy lives. As part of the retreat process, play and rest let people's minds absorb and digest what they heard and felt. The evening meal brought them back refreshed, ready for a gathering in the Great Hall, followed by singing with guitars, visiting, and a good night's rest.

Bill's retreats provided a trusting atmosphere for each person to look into his or her own life, to acknowledge the needs and difficulties, to feel the pain and other emotions, and to allow God's spirit to begin the healing. He witnessed honestly about his current struggles, and guests felt safe to look at their own lives and face their own difficulties. Bill became comfortable in this place of leadership. His gifts of hospitality and his people skills came together in his interaction with people. His personality proved to be natural for the work, and it was clear that God was with him in all of it. He studied the names of the people coming to each retreat, met them as they came down the path from the parking area, and called them by name from the moment they arrived. Working with a leader from the group coming in, he learned something of the special needs of each person and made himself available to those who were struggling.

The first evening meal was always delicious, easygoing, and comfortable. Bill's opening remarks in the Great Hall were warm and funny and created an atmosphere of trust and comfort. He told enough about himself to set everyone at ease, establishing an atmosphere of vulnerability that relaxed each anxious listener. He joked about the "heel tracks all through the gravel paths because some people had been dragged here by a well-meaning friend or spouse." Bill reassured these people. They did not have to attend anything they did not want to attend. They could even skip meals, he'd say, joking again.

Before he led the group in prayer, he often shared these verses: "Bless the LORD, O my soul, and all that is within me, bless His holy name. Bless the LORD, O my soul, and forget none of His benefits" (Ps 103:1-2). "In returning and rest shall you be saved; in quietness and in confidence shall be your strength" (Isa 30:15).

Set free by the leader, guests participated in almost every activity. Some fished, and some hiked or slept or read, testing the boundaries. After discovering they were really free, they usually came to the meetings. Bill was as non-threatening as a person could be. When the laughter rose to a roar, as it often did, everyone wanted to be part of the fun.

The retreats offered study, small groups, and play. By the closing day, most guests had developed a sense of community. The final morning brought an appetizing breakfast, one more teaching from the leader, or perhaps a witness. In the closing group session, each person chose one thing to take home to make his life or hers more pleasing to Jesus. Bill also taught guests how to go home from Laity Lodge. He gave guidelines for people who wanted to nurture their encounter with God. He shared ideas for how they might keep the energy moving in their lives in the coming days.

Almost every retreat closed with the Lord's Supper or Holy Communion, when those of different churches came together in the Lord. As the offertory, people shared what they had received during the retreat. A song together, a prayer together, and lots of hugs led into a final meal. We will never know all the far-reaching effects of the experiences individuals had at Laity Lodge. We do know that the rippling effects continue.

Though Bill provided guidelines for the sessions, no retreat was ever the same. Each was unique in its combination of people, leaders, and needs. And God was faithful in each gathering.

Howard and Barbara Dan Butt attended a great many of the retreats, and people always appreciated their presence. Howard's gifts as speaker and singer, plus his warm and cordial manner, added a great deal, as did Barbara Dan's good humor and sweet spirit. Participants came to know them both as private individuals and as the public hosts who made these retreats possible. Howard and Barbara Dan expressed their hospitality by treating each retreat as a "house party" in their country home and planned the amenities with that in mind.

Innovations and Additions

Across the years, Howard and Bill added new types of retreats to meet special needs. They initiated retreats for pastors, for Christian writers, for women, for men, for singles. In addition, national church boards and lay renewal organizations came to Laity Lodge. As needs came to Bill's attention, he designed ways to address them.

In addition to the garden and the new rooms under the Great Hall, Mrs. Butt Sr. initiated the building of Black Bluff and the Quiet House. Bill paid attention to every detail behind the scenes, including the food service and housekeeping. Bill also continued the "retreat within the retreat," as speakers and group leaders met with Bill to plan and pray throughout the retreat. Often these leaders brought their own needs and problems to the surface, and God ministered to them even as they worked with others. Many speakers came again and again because the time at Laity Lodge meant so much to them and to their families.3

Betty Anne said, "Centering on those years in this history of God's place called Laity Lodge, I think of certain words indicative of Bill's leadership: warmth, hospitality, acceptance, validity, integrity, stretching, growth, presence, community, witness, story, transparency, openness, service, family, and home."

Bill acknowledged that everything done was God's work. Bill's honesty invited the honesty of others, allowing everyone to acknowledge God's honesty and truth. Rooted firmly in his own faith, Bill could be open and accepting to a wide spectrum of beliefs in others. He believed that God meets us where we are right now, and he wanted to be at that meeting place with each person. He prayed that he would be available to serve in God's name, and God honored that prayer.

Notes

1 Betty Anne Cody wrote this chapter. It has been edited to fit the format of the book.

2 For example, the University of Indiana had begun work with small groups and had published a text on it.

3 A partial list of speakers during the Bill Cody years includes the following: Elton Trueblood led the first retreat and came several more times. Karl Olsson, Bruce Larson, and Ben Johnson were writing books and came to bring their ideas to Laity. John Claypool, Buckner Fanning, Browning Ware, and Warren Hultgren came from large church pulpits. John Newport, Wayne Oates, Myron Madden, and Findley Edge came from seminary faculties. Donn Moomaw, Gary Demarest, Lloyd Ogilvie, Earl Palmer, Don Williams, and Dale

Bruner came from the West Coast. James I. Packer, Bishop Goodwin-Hudson, and John Stott came from England. Edith Schaeffer and Elisabeth Elliot came for women's retreats. James Mallory, John King, Armand Nicholi, and Edward Thornton were among the popular teachers in the area of interpersonal relationships. Henri Nouwen came two times for weeks of study. Keith Hosey was among the leaders of contemplative prayer retreats and came many times. David Redding and Tom Howard were popular leaders for the creativity retreats. Jack Robinson, Ken Chafin, Creath Davis, Leighton Ford, and Lane Adams drew full retreats. Dancer Marge Champion and actress Jeannette Clift George led special weeks of celebration of creativity. For this larger group, the facilities of Linnet's Wings and Singing Hills were also used. There was praise, joy, and dancing in the canyon that week! The beloved Gert Behanna spoke for Alcoholics Anonymous and Al-Anon groups. So many others contributed so much to Laity Lodge. There is not room here to name them all, but each one made his or her contribution.

Chapter 6

Continuing the Dream: The Hovde Years

How I Met Howard Butt and Came to Laity Lodge

Howard Butt Jr. graduated from Baylor University in 1947, when he was nineteen years old. I entered Baylor in spring of 1948, just out of the navy. I went to a retreat before the fall quarter of school, and Howard Butt was the major speaker. I'd entered college planning to be a coach, but through his presentation, I felt the urging of God to go into the ministry. Every time Howard spoke at Baylor during my time there, he packed Waco Hall, and his presentations were unforgettable and life changing.

During my Baylor years, I had several conversations with Howard about a topic of mutual interest, basketball. My freshman year, I had walked on for tryouts a day late. Within three days, I found myself among seventeen (out of one hundred fifty) selected for the team, and I received a basketball scholarship for the next three years. As a sophomore, I played in Madison Square Garden for the NCAA semifinals. Two years earlier, Howard had attended the finals at Madison Square Gardens when Baylor played the University of Kentucky for the NCAA Championship. Howard and I crossed paths at the home of two older ladies, sisters involved with Baylor, who enjoyed having parties for players and fans after the basketball games.

Following graduation, I went to the seminary in Louisville, Kentucky, and majored in pastoral care under Wayne Oates, a pioneer in the field. After I received a Bachelor's degree in Divinity and a Master's in Theology, Dr. Oates encouraged me to go to Columbia University to study with Lank Osborne in the field of Family Life Education, where I received an Ed.D. While at Columbia, I had a wonderful experience starting a church in New Jersey filled with young engineers being trained by Bell Telephone Company to return to their communities as leaders.

After finishing the degree at Columbia, I began exploring one term foreign mission opportunities. In the 1950s, I traveled in the United States with a Japanese missionary, visiting Japanese churches of various denominations, to encourage those of Japanese descent to go to Japan. World War II had created a void there and an opportunity for missionary work. Next, my wife Carole and I discovered a need for foreign mission work in Liberia, West Africa, at a school called Rick's Institute. During our three years there, I taught the Bible and served as chaplain and coach, and Carole was dean of the women.

We were in Liberia when a friend, John Claypool, wrote us of his daughter's cancer. Feeling it was important to walk with him on this journey, we chose to move to Louisville to a church called Crescent Hill. John was the senior pastor, and I served as the counseling minister. John's daughter died a year later, and John received a call to be a senior minister at Broadway Baptist Church in Ft. Worth, Texas.

After I'd served as senior minister at Beechwood Baptist Church in Louisville for several years, I was invited to be director of a counseling center in Houston. Southern Baptist churches sponsored the Center for Counseling to provide a place where small churches could refer troubled members. The sliding fee scale made help available from a gifted staff at an affordable rate. Toward the end of that time, I told Carole I'd like to do something with a central focus on worship.

Two weeks later, Howard Butt Jr. called. John Claypool had recommended me for the position of director of Laity Lodge after I had filled in as a speaker there at the last minute. Howard and I dialogued for two months, and I accepted his offer to be the executive director of Laity Lodge in February 1, 1981—a position I held for eighteen and a half years until I retired in September 1999.

The Butts' Theology in Action

I quickly discovered that the theological focus of Laity Lodge was relational, stemming from the nature of the one God who reveals Himself in three persons and whose great desire is to reveal Himself and to relate to all His children. God has always existed as a relationship in the mysterious Trinity of the Father, Son, and Holy Spirit—one God who is love.

Mr. and Mrs. Butt Sr. taught their children that every single person was a well-loved child of God, valued and respected. This meant that the stockers, cashiers, guards, maintenance personnel, janitors, salesmen, drivers, warehouse personnel, and executives— all—were vital to the H-E-B stores' functioning. The three children accepted this vision of God and the world. They not only respected but also served a broad spectrum of people.

Here's an example of how the family lived out this truth. Three Mexican American women in their sixties came one day to the foundation offices. Eddie Sears, then the associate director of Laity Lodge, met them and asked how he could help. They said they were looking for Mrs. Butt. As they told more about why they wanted to see her, Eddie realized they were looking for Millie Butt, Mary Holdsworth Butt's sister-in-law. She had died recently.

Mrs. Millie Butt had apparently taught them in the fifth grade. They said, "When we were growing up, many people were unkind to us because we were Mexican American. Mrs. Butt treated us like real people, and we knew she cared for each of us." They explained, "It wasn't so much what she taught us as it was the way she treated us. We are Christians today because of the love that Mrs. Butt had for us." These women had come to the foundation offices hoping to see her and tell her how much she meant to them.

In *The Triumph of the West,* J. M. Roberts contends that the Judeo-Christian ethic has so penetrated the cultures of the world that everything is judged in its wake. A primary contribution of this ethic is an emphasis on the value of each individual, stemming from the relationship of profound respect that God has toward everyone.[1]

Each person has great value because each is a well-loved child of God. For a retreat ministry, this means that the relationships among staff members, the relationships of the staff to the guests, and the programming must reflect this God-centered view of the world. Jesus Christ insisted on relating to and loving everyone. This is one of the chief reasons he was put on the cross. Any person who insists on loving everyone will be in trouble with someone or some group, sooner or later. The Middle East, Korea, and Ireland produce stories of cruelty and misunderstanding for those who try to reach out in love. Closer to home, Native Americans, Africans, Hispanics, Caucasians, and Asians also know the pain hatred causes.

Yet we are called to love our neighbor. Richard Rohr said that the litmus test for the Christian is "the ability to respect the outsider."[2] How much we have grown in our life with Christ can be measured by whom we can love. One of the primary aims at Laity Lodge was to love each person as Christ loves us. As director, I encouraged all relationships in this kind of love.

An Atmosphere of Love

The relationships between staff members could be felt by the guests. The environment created by the relationships of the office staff, the foodservice staff, the housekeeping staff, the hostesses, and the foundation leadership spilled over into the overall retreat experience. Guests would have sensed competition. Instead, the loving staff members affirmed each other as a sign of the Spirit's presence. The work at Laity Lodge was such a joy for me because of the relationships that existed with all of the staff, the directors, and their spouses.

In the grocery industry the customer is the most important part of the business. In the same way, the guests are the most important part of the retreat business. We greeted each guest warmly. The first night as they congregated, one of the staff members embraced them with the words "Welcome Home." The hostesses did their best to meet the needs of every guest. As much as possible, every guest was affirmed, heard, and treated with respect. Continuing Bill Cody's tradition of the freedom of Laity Lodge, we made no effort to pressure the guests into attending the sessions. We learned to trust that God was equally present in the rooms, on the tennis court, on the dock, on the trails, and in the library. Trusting God to be active with every person was a part of the relationship that developed with the guests.

At the beginning of many retreats, the guests introduced themselves by telling their names, places of birth, and responses to questions like "How did you get your name?" "What is one thing you like about your family of origin?" "What would you like to get from this experience?" "Which child were you in your family?" Relationships among the guests began in this way.

Small Groups

We continued the Laity Lodge tradition from the early years of asking witnesses to bring their own stories and life experiences, sharing their Christian journeys with the guests so that guests could identify with them. Often guests went to the witnesses and talked about aspects of their own ragged edges. The guests and leaders also brought their concerns into the safety of small groups.

Vaclav Havel, former president of the emancipated Czech Republic, told of his experience growing out of a small group. "You can not live outside a culture. But you can create within it zones and spaces where you can become who you really are. It is in such places that you can speak the truth, where one can gather with others who share that truth." These places of truth continued in Czechoslovakia for years, growing in spite of the difficulty. He continued, "Over time, the truth became stronger and stronger, and at a certain point people began to walk in the streets and say to the system, 'We don't believe you any more.' And the system fell."[3] This haunting experience of Vaclav Havel gives strong evidence of the power to bring about personal and social change through a small, relational group.

Small groups had been a part of Laity Lodge since it began, and we continued the tradition. Guests can share things in a small group that they could never share in a larger group. During a weekend retreat, small groups usually met once or twice. Yet, it was astounding what transpired. Many people arrived carrying heavy burdens; others brought good news to share. The groups rippled with truth, laughter, and tears.

Most of the time, the small group agenda consisted of questions provided by the speaker. In the group introductions, people often shared a pressing personal difficulty or a joyful event to celebrate. We emphasized that small-group time was a time of caring, not curing—a sharing time, not an answer time. Sometimes the group unfolded in an unplanned way, and we encouraged leaders to remain open for the Holy Spirit to be at work transforming each person.[4]

On occasion, usually due to the dynamics of a retreat, we created small groups consisting of men and women separately. We encouraged members of the same family to find different groups. The church's minister or retreat planner selected the group leaders, a process that tended to work well. In almost every church that came to Laity Lodge, experienced group leaders accepted roles of small-group leadership with pleasure, eager to do at Laity Lodge what they had become experts at doing in their churches or vocations. Generally, the minister and staff did not facilitate a group, which allowed them a time of rest and renewal.

We designed the schedule to give everyone time to be with old friends and become acquainted with new people. Most people lack free time in their lives, and we left the afternoons unscheduled to give guests some critically needed space.

The Surroundings

Speakers, musicians, and guests stayed in Black Bluff, a beautiful stone building added during the Bill Cody years. Cantilevered over the river, this unique facility provides spacious and beautiful rooms, with a magnificent view of the river. Balconies between the rooms allowed retreatants to feel as if they were a part of the canyon.

In many rooms and throughout the grounds, Mrs. Butt Sr. had workmen engrave in tile and stone quotations from various poets. Mrs. Butt memorized volumes of poetry. Most conversations with her were punctuated with one of her favorite quotations, always affirming and inspiring. She named the rooms at Black Bluff after poets, with their words displayed at the doorways. Tennyson greeted guests with lines from the Prologue of *In Memoriam*:

> Strong son of God, Immortal love,
> Whom we that have not seen thy face,
> By faith, and faith alone embrace.
> Believing where we cannot prove....
> We have but faith we cannot know;

For knowledge is of things we see;
And yet we trust it comes from thee.
A beam of darkness: Let it grow.[5]

Dotting the grounds on large stones are other quotes, such as this
from Dostoevsky: "Be not forgetful of prayer. Every time you pray, if
your prayer is sincere, there will be new feeling and new meaning in it,
which will give you fresh courage. And you will understand that
prayer is an education."[6]

At Laity Lodge, the Butts made a conscious effort to create a relationship between the surroundings and the people, so that guests and
staff could see the world as created by God. Every pebble points to the
knowledge that we are all part of creation and well loved by God. The
Scriptures teach, "Dear friends, let us love one another, because love
comes from God. Whoever loves is a child of God and knows God.
Whoever does not love does not know God, for God is love" (1 John
4:7-8, "Today's NIV").

A Safe Place

In *The Message*, Psalm 61 says, "You've always given me breathing
room, a place to get away from it all, a lifetime pass to your safe house,
an open invitation as your guest." Finding a safe place is not the same
as cocooning, the American practice of fencing yards, locking win-
dows and doors, creating self-satisfaction and isolation.

Even a family in the throes of an argument can be a safe place if
love and commitment underscore the heated words. A safe place has
to do with interior stillness, though it may or may not have to do with
silence. Being safe means knowing that God speaks to the deepest part
of our souls, beyond our normal comfort zones. And God accepts us
without judgment.

From the beginning, providing a safe place has been high among
the priorities at Laity Lodge—a goal that continues today. The first
clue that the Laity Lodge experience will be different is the approach
to the property. From Highway 83, the entrance greets the visitor with
native stone, plants, and a cattle guard, but no gate. A dusty road leads
into the property, and the unpaved caliche gives the traveler a sense of

undisturbed nature, a sense that something unique will open in each guest's life because this is a place one can drop the mask and relax.

The road winds for half a mile, drops sharply downhill, then seems to dead end at the edge of the Frio River. A sign, suggested by Betty Anne Cody, reads, "Yes! You drive in the river." Texas ranchers may be accustomed to driving in the river, but almost everyone else in the world is startled to come to the banks and see no way across. We opened many retreats with a simple question, "What did you think when you drove into the river?" Responses included, "I opened the door and listened to the water," "I thought I might have a new experience with God," and "I felt like I was coming home."

Once guests emerged from the river and arrived at the lodge, the room situation continued to foster a feeling of safety. No keys were issued. Everyone was trusted: the guests coming to the center, the retreat staff, the maintenance employees, and the housekeepers.

I lock my car almost every place I go. I was robbed of a number of pieces of furniture I had in a van in a movie parking lot in San Antonio. Now, I lock my car at the grocery store, at the movies, at the tennis court, at church, and even in my driveway. We lock our homes out of habit.

No need for keys at Laity Lodge! We told the new arrivals that this space was trustworthy; they did not have to worry about someone breaking into their rooms or taking their belongings.

Laity Lodge offers a level of safety not available to most of us in our daily lives. Our guests could rest in the knowledge that their lives were not in danger if they went for a walk—day or night. Individuals who needed time to be by themselves could take it.

Besides offering physical safety, Laity Lodge offers emotional safety as well. Some guests arrived having been wounded by relationships, institutions, and circumstances. They felt unimportant. The major gathering room, the Great Hall, was designed with the gracious feel of a lovely living room, helping people know they are guests in a place that honors them. A welcoming space, the room itself made the wounded begin to feel safe and to become less guarded.

The philosophy of Laity Lodge includes keeping Christ in the center of all activities, giving a lofty place to Holy Scripture, and relating to each person as a fallible but well-loved child of God. One man came to Laity Lodge only because his wife wanted him to come. He spent most of the week on the fringes of everything. He did like the speaker, however, and toward the end of the week asked him, "Who are these people?"

Some people have a spiritual hunger, yet fear the church at the same time. They have learned through the years that church is not a safe place, especially to ask questions. A church member or a visitor may feel embarrassed for not knowing the Bible well; others fear the prospect of praying out loud. Some fail to meet the leader's expectations. Or a leader betrays their confidence. Some feel humiliated by a pastor, priest, or teacher. Some have been abused.

In a retreat environment, those old memories haunt us. Finding a safe place is like a great breath of fresh air. At Laity Lodge, we gave guests the freedom to participate in planned events or not participate—whatever would most assist them in their life journeys. God is present all over the property, not only in the Great Hall. He is the "Hound of Heaven,"[7] always after His children to bring them deeper, fuller lives. After all, God visited the man who kept to his room, hanging on the fringes. He showed Himself through the lack of pressure to attend the meetings. We always stated on the first night of the retreat, "The freedom of Laity Lodge is for you to do what you need to do to be blessed by God."

Small groups encouraged individuals to respect others by keeping their confidence. What was said there stayed there, and participants could talk—or not. Either choice was acceptable. I like to tell the story of a man in a small group I facilitated. He told us his name, where he was born, and where he lived. That was all. In the last group meeting of the weeklong retreat, I asked if anyone would like to pray. To our amazement the man prayed this prayer, "Lord, thank you for the people who can talk, so those of us who can't can learn in our silence."

Men and women attending Laity Lodge also know it is a safe place through the witnesses who share their closeness to God as well as the distance they have experienced from God—letting us in on their family histories, joys, and sorrows. At a men's retreat, I asked three men to use the following format: "Tell us about your relationships—

with God, the Father; with your own father; and with your children as their father. What does your commitment to Jesus Christ have to do with all these relationships?" We followed this general outline for men's retreats during the last five or six years I served as executive director. We did not advertise these as father/son retreats, but many brought their sons and sons-in-law. Family members trusted that others in their family would not be hurt by an experience at Laity Lodge.

We all need a safe place to ponder the primary questions of life. Who am I? Why am I here? Where is my life going? How can I deal with the bent fenders and ragged edges of my past? What can I do with my guilt, fear, or anxiety? Is God real? What must I do to meet God or to grow in my relationship with God? These questions require our attention if we are going to live fully. Finding a place to explore them in a trusting environment may be the finest gift we can give ourselves. Laity Lodge is such a place.

We have a loving God who cares for each of His children. This truth is the center of every Laity Lodge experience. Through the relationships among the staff, with the guests, and with the place itself, we tried to create a safe place where people could experience firsthand the knowledge and love of God.

Notes

1 J. M. Roberts, *The Triumph of the West* (Boston: Little, Brown, and Co., 1985) 72, 278.

2 Richard Rohr, *Everything Matters* (New York: Crossroads Publishing, 1999) 52.

3 Vaclav Havel, *Context* 34/7 (1 April 2002) 2.

4 See Appendix B for an excellent brochure on small groups, prepared by Barry Sweet and David Williamson.

5 Alfred, Lord Tennyson, *In Memoriam*.

6 Fyodor Mikhailovich Dostoevsky, *The Brothers Karamozov*, 1879.

7 Francis Thompson, *The Hound of Heaven*, 1889.

Chapter 7

At the Heart of the Dream: The Team

Behind the Scenes

"Getting to know you, getting to know all about you" are words from a song in the musical *The King and I.* Anna is singing to the children of the king of Siam, and the words describe the delight she experiences in loving and teaching them. The play tells of the transformation taking place in the whole, large family—including the king—due to the vision, wisdom, and love of their teacher. The children and the king catch the vision, making the whole country more alive and free.

Howard Edward Butt Sr. and his wife Mary Holdsworth Butt caught a similar vision. God gave them this vision, along with wisdom and love, and they shared it by creating Laity Lodge, the Free Camps, and the Laity Lodge Youth Camps. Howard Butt Jr., his wife Barbara Dan, their daughter Deborah Dan, and her husband David Rogers have carried on this ministry. David, with the deep, strong partnership of Deborah Dan, is taking on more and more responsibility in the leadership of all the programs of the H. E. Butt Foundation. They have taken up the dream and demonstrated the leadership gifts needed to guide the ministries of the foundation into the future. Like his father-in-law before him, David Rogers is learning to personify the organization's goals.

During our years at Laity, a strong team was essential to the smooth running of operations both during retreats and between sessions. As director, I felt called to infuse everyone working at Laity Lodge with the Butts' vision and dream in their work as well as to encourage an experience of God in their personal lives. Carole played her own role in this as she instigated and continued Bible studies, group meetings, and prayer time with the staff members. With fearful reluctance, the staff gatherings began. Though some were terrified of praying aloud, within six months, the sessions became the high point of the week for many. Relationships deepened, becoming more open and trusting. Carole knew the staff members' birthdays, wedding anniversaries, health issues, sorrows, and celebrations. Carole's strength and gentleness also blessed the staff and the guests at retreats. One of her special gifts is an alert, listening ear. Proverbs 20:5 says, "A person's thoughts are like water in a deep well, but someone with insight can draw them out." Carole's gentle presence drew out the thoughts of many. The workplace at Laity Lodge became a place of enrichment for all who worked there.

The Associate Director

On-site supervision can make the difference between a harmonious experience and one with an undercurrent of broken equipment, staff resentments, and other not-so-hidden problems. Eddie Sears, called by God from his grocery store through a holy unrest, became my colleague as associate director for nearly nineteen years at Laity Lodge. He said, "The hallmark of Laity Lodge since its first retreat in 1961 has been an emphasis on authentic hospitality. The Butt family's commitment to excellence, service, and unity is evidenced by everything that has been done at Laity Lodge, from the landscaping to the programs to the operational area."

Eddie brought a constellation of skills and gifts to his job. He started offering devotionals in the mornings before breakfast, for early risers to start the day steeped in the presence of God. Eddie created the jogging trail for exercise buffs and started line dancing at night in the Great Hall after the sessions were over. He supervised the staff, making sure that everything ran smoothly—no small task. A relational person, Eddie sat with people and talked during the whole conference. People found it easy to share with him, and these people remembered him for who he was, not for what he did.

During his time at Laity Lodge, Eddie helped the staff practice excellence in their work. He met with staff members, encouraged and affirmed them, and, most importantly, prayed with them. Through his leadership, his staff realized how important they were to the work of Laity Lodge. He said, "Everything at Laity Lodge has been done with one thing in mind: to allow the guests freedom from worry about these daily decisions so they might truly be present to the retreat process. It is when they are fully present to the retreat experience that they find time to explore their spiritual lives."

Eddie believed strongly in the "five-star legacy of authentic hospitality." I believed in it, too. Every director of Laity Lodge has. In fact, hospitality is one of the pillars of Laity Lodge's forty-year ministry.

Operations

Current director of operations, Tim Blanks, discussed his role in providing hospitality to those who come to Laity Lodge on retreat. "Hospitality means taking care of the creature comforts so the mind can be open to the experience . . . . It is like going to the home of a well-loved friend or relative." Tim recalled the story of a man moved by the generous nature of the staff. That man said, "My daughter would have been twenty-one today. Life is brief and fragile. I don't feel so lonely now. It is as if I was given a gift—a community."

When Tim was asked what his work has meant to him in his life with Christ, he responded, "I find that brokenness is a part of life. Rebirth is a grace from the bumps in the fenders. Brokenness can fill us with the power of the resurrection and help us live the Christian life with passion." He added, "My goal for next year is to help take the pressure off other people in the office. I want to help carry their burdens and make life lighter for them. I want to become a very good listener."

In a piece he wrote for me, Hugh Schneeman, assistant director of camp operations, unwrapped a bit of his life in the Frio Canyon. He remembered back in the late 1980s when he was trying his hand as a contractor without much success. A friend told him about a job possibility at Laity Lodge. The economy was sluggish, and he was hungry. So he agreed to work for a couple of weeks, which stretched into years. Hugh wrote, "When I first saw Laity Lodge, I was almost intimidated by its beauty. 'What a magnificent place,' I remember thinking. Even then I could feel there was something special about the whole establishment. You could sense the very soul of what that stupendous edifice was holding!"

For fourteen years, Hugh felt he was attending a continuous family reunion. "Laity Lodge was like going to heaven without having to pass through the Pearly Gates." In all the places he had worked before, time was money. And the end goal was also money. "The Butt family, their children, and grandchildren have a different perspective and believe that the end result should be a relationship with people. This philosophy is what Laity Lodge is all about—relationships." Hugh felt as though he were doing God's work in the world, a refreshing task . . . renewing, forgiving, inspiring. He concluded, "That's what Laity Lodge means to me! Being a part of accomplishing God's will."

The whole operation of maintenance in the Frio Canyon is a thing of beauty. During my tenure, it was done through the gifts of a compassionate servant leader whose spirit has permeated the whole staff. His name is Glenn Echols.

An example illustrates Glenn's quiet spirit. One of his crewmembers, an exceptionally strong, athletic powerhouse, had a reputation as a fighter. This crewmember told us in a staff meeting, "I used to beat up on anyone who crossed my path. But I don't do that anymore." He admitted he still had a difficult time controlling himself. "But the reason I don't fight anymore? I work with *him.*" He nodded toward Glenn.

How does Glenn, this gracious servant leader, live out the vision of Laity Lodge in his work? He explains it like this: "The mission of the operations team in the canyon includes providing a physically safe place for our guests. We care for the facility in a way that tells our guests we will care for them as well. We provide a physical atmosphere that is conducive to spiritual growth and reflection." Glenn nurtures the beauty of the canyon. He also strives to achieve a balance between the "values of excellence in stewardship and time with our families."

Glenn says, "When people feel cared for, they will be more open to the lessons that God wants to teach them during their time in the canyon. They are less defensive and more open to speakers, and they will experience the fellowship at a deeper level." He continues, "Our aim is to create an environment for the guests that will not be a distraction, but rather will assist them in focusing more on God's creation as expressed in the beautiful surroundings. Then they will be more able to hear His voice without all the clutter and clamor of their normal everyday world."

Glenn reveals another challenge: to call forth the gifts of the other members of his team. Each member had skills and talents. Some were obvious, but some were surprising, undiscovered gifts that needed to be called out through encouragement. For Glenn, creativity is one of the grand streams making his work a delight. "Utilizing the passions of each person means better work done and greater joy for everyone." Glenn describes work in the canyon as an intricate dance, critically necessary to produce the kind of atmosphere pleasing to God both in the physical plant and in the staff's attitude. He concludes, "Each staff person needs to see how their small, humble task results in people coming closer to the Lord. If they can keep this vision, they can hold on to the passion and joy of their work."

In the introduction to *The Soul of the Firm,* Bill Pollard articulates the management philosophy of Laity Lodge. Pollard talks about the soul of the cleaning firm he led. Though it does celebrate profits, it is a firm focused on "training and developing people." Although the employees toil at the mundane task of serving people by cleaning up after them, Pollard says, "We have basically reengineered jobs, provided training to people, and attempted to deliver a self-esteem that many workers have never had in the past."[1] The maintenance staff at Laity Lodge demonstrates this same vision in their work ethic.

A Laity Lodge Welcome

A Laity Lodge retreat begins with the initial contact by letter, e-mail, or phone. Every exchange influences our future guests' expectations. The retreat promises a sense of openness and acceptance and compassion. It promises a gentle unhurried pace of safety and trust. The welcome must confirm these expectations.

Dave Williamson, the current director of Laity Lodge, understands the importance of welcoming the guests. Since 1999, he has become an indispensable part of the Laity team. He realizes the retreat begins with the welcoming of the guests. Dave says, "The Laity Lodge program staff members are on hand to personally welcome the guests as they come down the walkway to the hostesses' office. We refer to the person who hands out room assignments and other important orientation information as a 'hostess' and not a 'registrar.' This person is part of the hospitality, and not an 'office' person." The difference in title designation translates into a special warmth toward the arriving guests. Little things reassure the guests—clean facilities, hot and cold beverages, and a big fruit bowl at the entrance to the dining room.

Linda Worden shared about her years of experience as a hostess at Laity Lodge. Hostesses, she said, need to have all the necessary materials in order. But they also need to be prepared emotionally and psychologically. They need a "manner that communicates care and kindness" to set the tone of the retreat. She continued, "The hostess must feel settled emotionally, ready to exude an aura of good will and genuine care. Guests arrive in a variety of states, and their moods will be greatly affected by the manner in which they are welcomed to the retreat."

Many Laity Lodge participants come from harried, over-committed work, home, and community involvements. They need the reassurance that they have arrived at a place where they are accepted, loved, and provided for. "The hostess' voice, mannerisms, preparedness, and calm demeanor assist in making guests feel safe and welcome," Linda said.

Food Service and Housekeeping

Even the food service and housekeeping have caught the vision of Laity Lodge. Bill Cody started the practice of introducing each member of the kitchen and housekeeping staff at the beginning of a retreat so the guests could interact with them. Staff and guests are part of the same family at Laity Lodge. Kathy Bort, a veteran of many years, said, "I love working at Laity Lodge. I feel very blessed to get to work at such a wonderful place with the staff of the whole Foundation Camp and the people at the office. It feels like one big family." Kathy's favorite job was serving in the dining room. "Some of the finest people in the world come to Laity Lodge, and as a server, I have the opportunity to meet them. Many have become my friends."

Another seasoned veteran, Linda Hortness, was the director of housekeeping for years. She said, "Working here helped me gain a faith in God I've never had before, and it's a good feeling." Throughout the years, Linda met many of the guests. Reactions to their stay at Laity Lodge varied. Many didn't want to leave. Or at the conclusion of the retreat, they were already planning when they might return. She saw many guests get emotional about leaving.

Linda continued, "I am especially fond of the remarks made about the housekeeping department, about how clean the rooms are. Guests are impressed by the great care given to Laity Lodge by so many of the staff. I know because I work with seven other ladies who take enormous pride in their work and in pleasing the guests with this gift of love." She appreciated the respect Mr. and Mrs. Butt show all the employees. "You don't get that working elsewhere. I thank God for this wonderful place. It is my second home."

Dora Canales, another employee of twenty years, added, "I enjoy working here because the company has been good to me in my time of service. I enjoy being around Christian people that come to the retreats. Presenting a nice, clean environment for them is a pleasure."

This all may sound ideal, even a bit unreal. Of course, Laity Lodge is not free of workday hassles, but how we deal with problems does make a difference. That's where we either live out our own philosophy—or not. For example, one morning after the guests arrived, Tom Kingery, former director of operations, asked whether a guest had a good night's sleep. She replied, "No. The bed is too soft, the sprinkler system that came on at 2:00 a.m. was too noisy, the sheets are too stiff, and the bedside light is too bright."

Tom was filled with a mixture of surprise, disappointment, and even anger. He said, "I couldn't believe anyone could miss the beauty of the place and focus on seemingly minor discomforts. But I was wrong. That event actually made me understand a different view of the word 'hospitality.'" Our guests and staff are not all the same. They come to retreats with every imaginable temperament, expectation, resentment, hurt, joy, bewilderment, fear, anger, and love. As it turned out, this person had recently experienced the loss of a beloved spouse of thirty years. Over the experience of the retreat, she was able to journey into her grief, sense the terrible loss, experience a supportive community, and begin to accept the safety and love God provides.

Tom said, "Hospitality comes in many packages. Well-groomed grounds, fresh sheets, good food, spotlessly clean rooms, strong speakers, and great music and art. It also comes through people who will care, listen, love, pray, laugh with you—and make you feel blessed."

On the Web

One final member joined the team during my tenure. Dan Roloff came on board in 1985 and has continued to broaden the Laity Lodge ministry through his role as publishing manager. When he first joined the foundation staff from the Youth Camp in the mid-nineties, the Internet was in its infancy. He added a new dimension to Laity Lodge through the World Wide Web, saying, "A presence on the web is a necessity for any successful retreat center."

Dan provided an online brochure, offering people an opportunity to see the facilities and to check the schedule for future retreats. "Our home page is www.hebuttfdn.org," he explained. "From this address we link to all our various programs."

The mission of Laity Lodge is pure poetry:

> The renewal of society through the renewal of the Church;
> Church renewal through renewal of the family;
> Family renewal through renewed individuals.

In conjunction with this mission, Howard Butt and Dan Roloff developed another Internet website to reach out to individuals in the ordinary circumstances of their lives. Howard's vision for the vital role of the laity in the church and daily life has led him to write several books and produce one-minute radio messages titled *The High Calling of Our Daily Work*. Dan commented, "TheHighCalling.org offers users a tool to delve deeper into the concepts introduced in those radio messages, connecting people with faith that undergirds and sustains all that we do." The site offers audio messages of encouragement and inspiration, along with Bible studies and narrative pieces that reflect on the same themes, relating them to ordinary circumstances of life. Recently, *Christianity Today* began repackaging the same content for a new audience at FaithInTheWorkplace.com.

One of the great pleasures of my job at Laity Lodge was working with a team of people committed to the vision of the H. E. Butt Foundation. Each member takes his or her job seriously. Maintenance crews and supervisors, hostesses, cooks, servers, housekeepers, fundraisers, vice presidents, webmasters, and everyone else involved serve God and make the Laity Lodge experience meaningful. From every quarter of the H. E. Butt Foundation staff come bright, clear reflections of the vision, creating a philosophy of work with Christ at the center. I can imagine God viewing the whole enterprise and smiling warmly.

Note

1 Bill Pollard, *The Soul of the Firm* (Grand Rapids MI: Zondervan, 1996) 13.

Chapter 8

Special Features of the Dream: Art, Music, Books, and Beauty

The Gift of Art

God encourages us through everything that is true and beautiful. Several years ago, Carole and I took a once-in-a-lifetime journey to France. In Paris we saw a painting by Eugene Burnand at the Musée d'Orsay titled *The Disciples Peter and John Running to the Sepulchre on the Morning of the Resurrection.* We spent nearly an hour looking at this masterpiece. Soon we felt bathed in the presence of God. We shared the awe and wonder on Peter and John's faces as they ran that day. We shared their anticipation of seeing Jesus alive and victorious.

Interest in the arts at Laity Lodge began under Keith Miller and Bill Cody and grew during my time as director. But what, exactly, do the arts have to do with Laity Lodge's mission of renewal?

Ginger Geyer, a former museum curator and gifted ceramics artist, became involved with the Laity Lodge Cody Center, serving as part-time consultant. She wrote, "Anyone who has delved deeply into creative endeavors senses those moments when time stands still, and it seems as though they are being helped by hidden hands. At Laity Lodge, we recognize this as the enabling, affirming work of the Holy Spirit." Participation in the arts helps people become more aware of this vivifying presence. For many people, artistic creativity provides profound refreshment; for others, it provides painful but necessary awareness. Either response leads to renewal.

Ginger observed that the arts help us to deploy our imaginations, to regain our childlike sense of wonder. Experiencing music, painting, poetry, and pottery alongside verbal teaching helps the message sink in. The arts give us a fresh look at specific Bible stories; moreover, they reveal the overarching ecumenical truth of the Scriptures. For those steeped in sacramental and mystical traditions, the arts reveal the holy in the ordinary, God's presence in our everyday world. For those who stress the immanence of God, the arts enlarge the capacity for transcendence and awe. When guests take these experiences home and share them with family and friends, their community grows toward more inclusive compassion.

We based our philosophy of the arts on the Bible. Matthew Fox relates the biblical teaching on creativity: every human being is endowed with the divine power of birthing, an essential belief if we are to redeem the words "art" and "artist" from an elitist and human-centered culture. "The artist in each one of us needs to be let out of the closet. It deserves to be shared, to be wondered at, to be celebrated. . . . Where art is recovered as an essential human activity, ecstasy returns."[1]

We are children of God made in God's image. When we grasp that truth, our souls stand tall. God transforms our vision of ourselves.

He can use anything to reach our hearts. A wide variety of art forms have been a part of the creative life of Laity Lodge: creative writing, painting, sketching, hymn writing, jewelry making, birdhouse building, calligraphy, fabric art, guitar, leather craft, flower arranging, book making, acting, cooking, pottery, journal keeping, picture book design, photography, stained glass, basket making, liturgical dance, knitting, quilting, puppet making, and bead work. Laity Lodge started offering creativity weeks each summer to help guests worship God through art. These retreats often fill up quickly and have wait lists.

Almost everyone has some artistic gifts, hidden or known. One of my early efforts at drawing tells a story. I had started a pencil drawing and was so excited with it that I ran to my mother to show her my work. She might have said, "I am so glad you like to draw," or "Isn't it exciting to see the wonderful design you made?" Instead, she asked, "That is interesting, Howard. What is it?" Then I looked more carefully at my prize. "I thought it was a man, but I guess it looks more like a potato!" And yet, I wasn't discouraged. The results didn't matter to me because the process of drawing brought me such joy. That is the delight of art.

At Laity Lodge, we say, "Art isn't a product; it is a process." Part of that process is the community that develops when individuals create something side by side. Prying guests away from their projects even for a meal becomes a challenge. They are having such fun that artwork seems more like play. They share their thoughts while they work. They have heart-to-heart conversations. Frequently, God helps budding artists find healing as they share some of the light and darkness they have experienced.

Dr. George Smith, an ear, nose, and throat doctor from Jackson, Mississippi, was surprised when he began to bring life out of a lump of clay. He had dealt with the head and neck his whole medical career. As he held the clay in his hands, he saw the unity of the human body for the first time. He said, "I am convinced every medical student should be given the opportunity to do this. It would help every one."

Dr. Sherman Coleman was a gifted and distinguished surgeon. His wife Jackie, a sculptor, urged him to make something with a lump of clay. He was not inclined even to try. Finally, he took a bit of time and shaped a foal. He said, "I think I can really do that!"

Today, his sculptures dot the landscape of his home community of Corpus Christi. One of his huge bronze horses stands on Ocean Drive. He sculpted *Rejoice with Me*, an eight-foot bronze shepherd holding up a lamb outside the Church of the Good Shepherd. *Christ the Healer*, a collaboration between Sherman and his daughter, Kathleen, welcomes visitors with open arms to the Spohn Hospital in south Texas.[2]

Both Sherman and his daughter have taught during Creativity Week. In honor of Howard Butt's ministry, Sherman sculpted the statue of the boy shepherd with three sheep located in the meadow just below the gazebo. Titled *A Safe Place*, it greets all who come to Laity Lodge.

Music

We love music at Laity Lodge. Music gives hints of God's mystery and opens our hearts to Him. Singing praises brings us closer to God. In the *Good News Bible*, Psalm 149 begins, "Sing a new song to the Lord; praise him in the assembly of his faithful people!" In Psalm 150, the psalmist adds all available instruments to the joyous expression of adoration:

> Praise him with trumpets.
> Praise him with harps and lyres.
> Praise him with drums and dancing.
> Praise him with harps and flutes.
> Praise him with cymbals.
> Praise him with loud cymbals.
> Praise the Lord, all living creatures!
> Praise the Lord.

All retreats at Laity Lodge incorporate music—both singing and different kinds of instruments. I remember one retreat in particular. Everyone singing together and offering praise in the Great Hall with "Christ, We Do All Adore Thee." The music seemed to cleanse my body, and I was physically shaken by its beauty. I felt like Richard in George MacDonald's *The Baron's Apprenticeship*: "In the crowd waiting more than an hour at the door of the orchestra to secure a seat for a shilling, no one knew so little of music as he. But the first throbbing flash of the violins cleft his soul as lightning cleaves a dark cloud and set his body shivering as with its thunder—and lo, a door was opened in heaven."[3]

The universal language, music speaks to us from every height and depth of life. Stephen Clapp, dean of the Juilliard School, concludes most of his violin concerts at Laity Lodge with "It Is Well with My Soul." Horatio G. Spafford wrote that moving hymn when he was on the way to the funeral of his wife and four daughters. He lost all five of them when their ship sank in the Atlantic. I cannot imagine anything worse for a parent to suffer. In the midst of such terrible suffering, Spafford wrote, "Whatever my lot, Thou hast taught me to say, 'It is well, it is well with my soul' . . . Praise the Lord, praise the Lord, O my soul."[4]

God uses all kinds of music to awaken our spirits. Bach and Beethoven, Taize chants, classical hymns, short choruses, contemporary songs, Scripture songs: each can touch us and make us aware of God's constant presence. Music says our prayers for us. Like the Holy Spirit who prays for us when we cannot find the words, music brings our souls to life. Another one of George MacDonald's characters says, "I can't pray at all sometimes till I get my fiddle under my chin, and then it says my prayers for me till I grow able to pray."[5]

God graces us with moments that gently lift our spirits into life. Such a moment came to me, during the music, one stormy night at Laity Lodge when the world seemed made of lightning. Every brilliant flash was accompanied by pounding thunder that shook the Great Hall. David Tolley, pianist and composer, asked that the lights be turned out. Amidst the blazing light and God's own, resounding cymbals, he played "The Phantom of the Opera," and we experienced a taste of God's power and majesty. As I sit and write this recollection, even the memory of that experience calls Him forth again.

The freedom and safety of Laity Lodge inspired amazing creativity for some.

Like Madeleine L'Engle. For ten years she spent a month each year at Laity Lodge and wrote undisturbed each morning in her room.

Like Eugene Peterson. He first discovered his gift for transliteration at Laity Lodge. His wife, Janice, shares the story with everyone. He was just a quiet college professor, but his friends convinced him to share a psalm during an open reading one evening. The room was stunned. "He would never have written *The Message* if it were not for Laity Lodge," Janice says. Like Madeleine L'Engle, he wrote many portions of it while living at the lodge for weeks at a time.

Like Kathy Ellis. Laity has been pivotal to her music. A pianist and composer, she wrote a "Fugue" for Madeleine L'Engle after their second retreat together. Kathy said, "I have been blessed by Laity Lodge over and over, and I want you to know I'm grateful."[6]

Stories from Creativity Week

Charles Webb, dean emeritus of the Indiana University School of Music, led a class during Creativity Week. We all expected to learn the background of some of the great hymns of the faith. And we did, but he added a big surprise. He said, "Now everyone in the class will write a hymn!" We lost a third of the students. Most of us were not music majors. Composing a hymn was not even on the screen of our imaginations. But everyone who stayed wrote a hymn, fifteen in all. We bound them into a small hymnal as an offering to God and each other.[7]

One night during most creativity retreats, the guests put on a talent show. It is a grand adventure when gifted people create art as gifts to each other, whether poetry, singing, acting, skits, stories, or instrumental numbers.

Musicians and artists often bring their spouses when they come to perform or teach. Including their spouses is an important ministry to the artists. It helps them become part of the total experience. We ask our musicians to offer a concert, but they are not merely performers. They lead us in worship and make presentations at most gatherings of the group.

Surprise blossoms in the hearts of the guests at Laity Lodge. Sometimes the person most affected by a retreat is one of the leaders or artists. Corey Cerovsek was born in Vancouver to a Romanian father who had been disowned for marrying a gypsy. Corey developed so slowly that his parents thought he was retarded. However, when they put a violin in his hands, they found that they were raising a genius in their home.

Corey attended Indiana University at age twelve. At fifteen, he received his Bachelor's degrees in music and math. At seventeen, he earned his Master's in music and math, and at nineteen, he earned Ph.D. degrees in both disciplines! The math department found him a rare, original thinker. The music department agreed. Corey was also one of the few people who could play a very difficult composition on the violin and, without leaving the stage, play an equally difficult work on the piano.

At age fifteen, he came to Laity Lodge during Creativity Week and was drawn to make a leather belt with a silver buckle. It went so well he decided to make one for his father. He finished the second leather belt but did not have time to finish a second silver buckle. On the night of "graduation," everyone displayed their artwork in the Great Hall. Before dinner, Corey laid his belt on the table, next to the incomplete belt for his father.

When he returned to the Great Hall after dinner, he was amazed to find a shining silver buckle on his father's belt. Jim Morris, the teacher of the class, had completed Corey's gift.

Two weeks later we received a letter from Corey's mother. His father, who did not have an easy time with a genius for a son, was moved by Corey's gift. Corey's mother told us that Laity Lodge had given her son four of the finest days of his life.

Another Creativity Week brought us Alexander Ginzburg, a confidante of Aleksandr Solzhenitsyn in Russia. Ginzburg had been entrusted to give money from Solzhenitsyn's books to family members of dissidents whose jobs had been taken from them. Because aiding dissidents' families was illegal, Ginzburg carried all the addresses in his memory. Everyone who helped Solzhenitsyn distribute money was incarcerated. Ginzburg was no exception. In fact, he endured prison twice. He'd finally been freed from his second prison term in an international exchange for Russian prisoners.

When he arrived in America, he wore clothes designed to keep a man warm in a Russian winter. It was June in south Texas. Friends soon found him weather-appropriate clothing. He gave his first U.S. speech in clear but halting English. When asked how he could possibly endure two prison terms, he said the days were difficult. Yet, far more horrible than the days were the screams of his friends as they were tortured.

During the week at Laity Lodge, Alexander made many gifts for his new friends. He befriended Henry Parish, the tennis pro, and in clay molding class he made Henry a ceramic tennis ball. He took it to the courts to give the gift to Henry but was unable to go inside the fence. There were too many bad memories.

Late in the afternoon of the last day, Kathleen Edwards, a bronze artist and teacher, displayed ten of her magnificent bronzes near the walk leading to the dining room. Alexander came to admire them. Kathleen asked him which one he liked the best: a head of Christ, an Indian maiden, a Brave, a whale with its calf swimming in kelp, or one of the others. He examined each of the ten pieces carefully. He went down the whole row and returned slowly and pensively. Stopping, he pointed to the whales.

Kathleen said, "It's yours."

He looked toward her and back at the sculpture. "Impossible!" he blurted.

"Only if you will not receive it," she replied.

Somewhere in France today, that piece graces the home of one of the twentieth century's unsung heroes.

Books at Laity Lodge

My parents were avid magazine readers. Primarily they read *Reader's Digest, Saturday Evening Post, Redbook, Good Housekeeping,* and *Sports Afield.* As a child, my mother often read books to my brother and me, books like Stephenson's *Garden of Verse, Black Beauty, Call of the Wild,* and *Charlotte's Web.*

Growing up, I soaked up some of the books, but my father and I each had another passion—sports. That interest consumed me more than reading. Though I had exceptionally good English teachers in high school, a Baylor University professor helped reveal the void I had in my knowledge of books. Paul Baker, chairman of the Drama Department, had biked all over Europe and Russia at sixteen to explore live theaters. I took his class, "The Integration of Personality." Over the course of the semester, he stretched us and opened our minds to see our latent talents by requiring that we act and write music, poetry, and prose.

One revealing exercise he gave us was a challenge to name ten professional basketball, ten football, and ten baseball players. That was not a problem for me. Then he asked us to name ten American writers, ten artists, and ten poets. When all of us failed almost totally, he said, "I hate to tell you this, but you are all ignorant." I was trapped in the tiny world of my own thoughts and ideas. Paul Baker showed me the larger world to which books could lead me.

George Steiner, Cambridge Fellow and English professor at the University of Geneva, wrote that nothing can replace the inner dialogue sparked by reading. "A book can always accompany you, it will grow with you, it will change with you. It is surely the indispensable companion." He says people continue to labor at writing books because they know somewhere, someone might pick up that book and "it will change their life."[8]

Joy Davidman fell in love with the writings of C. S. Lewis. She fell in love with God through Lewis's books. Then she fell in love with Lewis himself and became his wife. A former atheist and communist, Joy wondered how many others like herself would still be in darkness if it wasn't for the writings of C. S. Lewis.

Most of us have been introduced into a larger world by some book, such as *Good Night Moon, The Secret Garden, The Chronicles of Narnia,* or *A Wrinkle in Time.* Even with the electronic world calling to get our attention, it is still a reader's world. In 2003, book sales reached around 650 million.

Retreat attendees are more likely to be readers than the general population, and the Laity Lodge bookstore plays an important role in each retreat. In addition, the Butt family members were all avid readers, and Howard Butt Jr. is also an author. Three of his works include *The Velvet Covered Brick, Renewing America's Soul,* and *Who Can You Trust?: Overcoming Betrayal and Fear.*

Some find books a means of encouraging individuals toward a faith in Jesus Christ. Charles Colson, of Watergate fame, was one. Just before the government's Watergate cover-up broke, he went to see an old friend, Tom Phillips, CEO of Raytheon, for comfort and encouragement. As he was leaving, Tom gave him a copy of *Mere Christianity* by C. S. Lewis. Then Tom prayed for his friend. Charles didn't believe in God at the time, but he sensed Tom's freedom. Afterward, he wept in his car in Tom's driveway. Later, he took a weeklong vacation to be with his wife and study Lewis's book.

Colson writes in *Born Again,* "I opened *Mere Christianity* and found myself face-to-face with an intellect so disciplined, so lucid, so relentlessly logical that I could only be grateful I had never faced him in a court of law." A week later Charles Colson accepted Christ.[9] His conversion to Christianity resulted in a prison ministry that has encouraged thousands of imprisoned men and women to become new people in Jesus Christ.

The book ministry at Laity Lodge grew exponentially during my time as director. In 1983 we had outgrown the original bookstore and moved into a larger space. Every retreat we introduced the group to new and classic Christian authors. Eddie Sears or I would pick up several books from the bookstore and tell a little bit about each one, hoping to pique the interest of people hungry to read and hungry for God. By the time I left, the bookstore had outgrown its walls again. It is a continuing dilemma. A larger space could house more books. On the other hand, a small space requires careful selection of books. Narrowing the options has become in itself a gift to our guests. After every retreat, I returned to the bookstore to find where the books slanted on the shelves; that told me what books people had bought and which ones I needed to reorder.

Because Laity Lodge is interdenominational, the books in our store represent a wide variety of authors. The vision of the retreat center gives direction to the choices of books.

Where did I begin with books to recommend? I remember challenging a group at Laity Lodge to read a devotional classic, when Madeleine L'Engle, the retreat leader, broke in. "Tell them to read the Bible and to read it from the beginning to the end. Most of us don't know what's in there." The Laity Lodge bookstore features several translations. We even helped inspire one! Our bookstore proudly offers Eugene Peterson's *The Message.*[10]

In *Renewing America's Soul,* Howard Butt Jr. says there are "three perennial resources, three sources of fixedness offering us constancy and courage: Scripture, Prayer, and The Church." Of the Scriptures he wrote, "To soak in the Scriptures is modern humanity's greatest need."

Books have a power to touch our heads and hearts. They can be an effective means of helping us meet God and deepen our lives with Christ, experience pure delight, have fun, evangelize, receive gifts, and learn truth.

The Gift of Beauty

God expresses Himself through creation and beauty. His beauty sur-
rounds us, and the more we grow in God's grace, the more we
recognize His beauty in the world around us. At Laity Lodge we
believe that beauty is a reflection of God. That is why we place a primary value on aesthetics.

Laity Lodge is alive with beauty. From the Hill Country gate to
the drive in the pure, clear water of the Frio River, Laity Lodge speaks
beauty's mysterious language. Landscaped in Hill Country style, the
grounds sing God's praise. The plants and trees clap their hands for
God. John Calvin liked to think of the natural world as a theater of
God's glory, where the drama unfolds.[11]

At Laity Lodge, the tennis courts had their special place in beauty's
parade. The man who most graced the courts, Henry Parish, had been
the national seniors' tennis champion in both singles and doubles. His
grace and beauty impressed every opponent, whether he was playing
an outstanding college student or a person taking a racket in hand for
the first time. Sometimes he challenged four, six, and even eight players at a time! His goal then was not competition, just the pure joy of
the game. Henry often stops a game to watch the vultures soar, or to
listen to a cardinal or canyon wren, or to see a blazing sunset. And
because of his love for God, the courts are called "Henry's Chapel."

The stone and wood buildings of Laity Lodge blend into the landscape as naturally as the wildlife. The rooms speak of special care by
the quality of the carpeting, furniture, blinds, shutters, and lighting.
The housekeeping staff makes the beds in the morning while the participants meet in the Great Hall. The care they give the rooms is a gift
of beauty. The Great Hall spreads an ambiance of welcome, warmth,
quiet, peace, and God.

The vision of the Butt family has provided another gift of beauty:
an intimacy created by the limited number of participants. They
wanted a place that would contain and care for a total of seventy-two
people, including staff, speakers, artists, and musicians. This number
gave the guests a sense of proportion, allowing enough, but not too
many, new faces. The balance of people at each retreat became a thing
of delight.

Cardinal Gottfried Daneels, archbishop of Mechelen-Brussels, Belgium, says this: "The contemporary Westerner hesitates before the True, is impotent before the Good, but loves Beauty." Daneels continues, "I ask myself whether we are using sufficiently one of the doors that lead to God—the door named Beauty. Indeed, God is Truth, Holiness is Moral Perfection, but God is also Beauty."12

The Bible uses many words for beauty: honor, majesty, desire, fairness, appearance, sight, pleasantness, ornament, and form. In Psalm 96 in *The Message*, the psalmist celebrates God's beauty: "God made the heavens—Royal splendor radiates from him, A powerful beauty sets him apart. Bravo, God, Bravo! Everyone join in the great shout: Encore!"

God's saints can see His beauty in everything. Once we welcome the presence of God into our awareness, the world becomes alive with unspeakable beauty. At Laity Lodge we pray that God will open our guests' eyes to Himself through beauty, so they might take God home and see Him there.

Opportunities for creativity at Laity Lodge become a source of beauty—when people discover previously unexpressed gifts they carry, or when their love for art deepens. Beauty grows in the amphitheater and winds down the hillside. The Cody Center seems to have grown from the earth where architects revealed it in perfect symmetry. Beauty emanates from the speakers, who come from many parts of the Christian family and pour out the wisdom of their hearts. More beauty grows within the small groups, where people share their personal life adventures. One man, the CEO of a small company, told his small group that he went to work thirty minutes before any employees arrived to prepare for the day. Amazed, he told the group God had opened in him a new consciousness. Before Laity Lodge, it had never occurred to him to invite God into that time. Life suddenly became more beautiful for him.

Dr. Wendy Wright says, "The absence of beauty is a profound form of deprivation."13 Studies have shown that people deprived of beauty turn to violence. Too many people go through life deprived of beauty. A Laity Lodge retreat provides them with at least one beauty-filled experience. At Laity Lodge, we see beauty in people at rest in hammocks and in others sharing a swing with a spouse or a friend. We find loveliness walking by the river at night when the stars seemed unusually close, and singing echoes against the canyon walls.

Dostoevsky meant all of this and more when he said, "Beauty will save the world." Every retreat at Laity Lodge brings as much beauty to guests as their hearts will allow. God is the source of all beauty, and we can never get enough of God.

Notes

1 Matthew Fox, *Original Blessing* (Santa Fe NM: Bear and Co., 1983) 184-86.

2 The results of Sherman T. Coleman's artistic abilities are most notably *Rejoice with Me* at the Church of the Good Shepherd,

Christ the Healer at Christus Spohn Hospital on Shoreline, *The Legend of the Sand Dollar* at the entrance to the Corpus Christi Museum, and *Captain Alonzo de Pineda* at de Pineda Park, all in Corpus Christi, Texas.

3 George MacDonald, *The Baron's Apprenticeship* (Minneapolis: Bethany House, 1986) 164.

4 Used by permission.

5 George MacDonald, *The Shopkeeper's Daughter* (Wheaton IL: Victor Books—SP Publications, 1986) 212.

6 Written in a letter to Don Murdock, executive director of Laity Lodge, 29 April 2002. Used with permission.

7 Many guests wrote psalms and hymns during Creativity Week. In Appendix A, I have included some of the psalms and hymns I wrote.

8 George Steiner, *Times Literary Supplement* 1/12 (27 April 2002).

9 Charles Colson *Born Again* (Old Tappan NJ: Chosen Books, F. H. Revell Co., 1976) 121.

10 Some of the authors represented in the Laity Lodge bookstore are as follows: C. S. Lewis, Madeleine L'Engle, Howard E. Butt, Jr., Frederick Buechner, Paula D'Arcy, Paul Tournier, Leslie Williams, Thomas Howard, Jeanie Miley, Betsy Rockwood, Bitsy Rubsamen, Earl Palmer, John Claypool, Barbara Brown Taylor, Roberta Bondi, William Temple, Reinhold Niebuhr, Karl Barth, Dale Bruner, Douglas Steere, Keith Miller, Richard Rohr, David Redding, Thomas Kelly, Robert Slocum, Dorothy Sayers, Charles Williams, and Bob Buford. In addition, the bookstore stocks Christian classics by Augustine, Thomas á Kempis, St. Teresa of Avila, St. John of the Cross, Thomas Merton, Evelyn Underhill, Francois Fenelon, Soren Kierkegaard, William Law, John Woolman, John Calvin, John Wesley, George

MacDonald, John Donne, Meister Eckert, Rufus Jones, Leo Tolstoy, Fyodor Dostoevsky, G. K. Chesterton, and John Bunyan.

11 Martin Marty. *Context* 34/4 (15 February 2002): 5

12 Gottfried Daneels. *Context* 33/20 (15 November 2001): 6-7.

13 Wendy Wright at a North American Retreat Directors Association (NARDA) Conference in Daytona Beach, Florida, 1-2 March 2002.

Chapter 9

Memories of the Dream: Testimonies from Laity Lodge

This chapter includes stories from people whose lives were changed at Laity Lodge. 1

Ginny and Ralph Berkeley

Ginny, a woman from Houston, wrote, "I should have suspected that an adventure awaited me when I first saw the sign, 'Yes! You drive in the river!' The fact that there were no markers in the water for guidance was another clue to the unexpected that awaited us at Laity Lodge." She added that a subtle and deep awareness whispered to her, "A divine orchestration is unfolding behind the scenes."

She continued, "I could not sit in the Great Hall with its laughter and its healing tears without feeling that great arms of love were about me. I had been on an artificial respirator emotionally all my life. The oughts and shoulds of my family and my culture had stifled most of the airways of my existence." At Laity Lodge, something or someone deep within her began to live for the first time. She began to take deep breaths of fresh air into those closed airways. "Each journey to Laity Lodge increased this awareness of aliveness."

Ralph, her husband, said, "Somewhat against my will, I went to Laity Lodge in the summer of 1970. I had not had the foresight to make other vacation plans and was stuck with my wife's plan to go on a retreat. Ginny did want to go, and I decided another 'return to nature' experience couldn't be that bad. At least it would cure her of ever wanting to go again."

Ralph and Ginny came to that first retreat during a difficult time in their lives, as they suffered through the grief and uncertainty of a growing problem facing one of their children. Ralph was a person of faith, but as the problem deepened, he often wondered, "Where is God? What can I do?" He approached Laity Lodge with these questions.

The week turned out to be pleasant, but not in the way he expected. Ralph came from a West Texas pioneer family. In that culture, a man stood straight with his chin up regardless of external circumstances. The idea of sharing feelings was unmanly, a violation of an unspoken code. A profession of religious faith was acceptable as long as it was brief and not accompanied by unseemly emotion. He said, "West Texans are strong people and I am proud of my heritage. They gave me much of what I am today, but at this time I was suffering emotional pain and had no tools to cope with my problems."

After a day at Laity Lodge, Ralph was awash with feelings and, thanks to Bill Cody, he found a safe place to express them. Bill had a way of reading the crowd, and on the second day of the retreat, he asked Ralph a pointed question about his spiritual condition. They talked and Ralph opened up. "And it was okay. I was forty years old, I shared, and it was okay. For the first time in my life, I felt I could share all aspects of my life and be heard in a loving, nonjudgmental atmosphere. I began to understand the Christian walk in a way I had not seen."

Ralph concluded, "The Butt family responded to the call of God and lives have changed, are being changed, and will be changed. Now this ripple cascades through persons, families, and the Church of Jesus Christ. This thought makes me deeply grateful and deeply happy."

Norma Duff

Norma, a woman from Odessa, Texas, wrote, "My first time at Laity Lodge came from my search for a way to bring my young children into a closer walk with God." Her family was active in church, but it seemed she always wanted more. "Someone recommended a book, *The Taste of New Wine* by Keith Miller. I bought it and was gripped by it. What most caught my eye was his mention of a place called Laity Lodge. I had no idea what laity meant."

Norma and her friend took their daughters to the youth camps at Laity Lodge. Then they drove to the lodge itself, where they sat down on the porch and explained to Bill Cody that they *had* to stay. He said there was a house up the road called Lodestar, but the air conditioning was out. It was July in the Hill Country, and the room would be an oven. Norma and her friend had no clothes other than those they were wearing. They told Bill they would stay, that they loved hot weather, and the heat would not bother them!

Norma said, "If Bill Cody had not seen our hearts and our need to find God and had sent us away, we would never have known the gifts God had for us. Because of Laity Lodge, my husband and I have had thirty-five years of a closer walk with Jesus. We will always remember the gifts Bill gave us. Particularly, he always pointed us to Christ."

Robert Sohn

Robert Sohn was driving through Hunt, Texas, on the scenic but winding road to Laity Lodge for his first visit, and his mind was racing. "It was the early 1970s, and though I thought of myself as careful, confident, well-educated, and assertive, in retrospect I know I was lost. Though I couldn't express it in words, I was yearning for meaning in my life."

It was raining lightly, and the road was wet enough to be dangerous. Lost in thought and driving at what turned out to be excessive speed, Robert lost control of his car and skidded across the highway. He and his car—miraculously undamaged—almost careened off the road into the Guadalupe River.

Shaking and quivering with fear, he backed away from the edge and drove on to the riverbed entrance that led to Laity Lodge. He made it, but the terrifying journey had riveted his attention.

He said, "I was immediately struck by the warmth of the staff's greeting. No one there knew me previously, but I was embraced and greeted, both by the place and by the people, as if I was family; as if I belonged there; as if I had known them all my life. It was almost as if I had come home."

Robert had heard the words "unconditional love" thousands of times, but never before had he been greeted and immediately accepted with that kind of love. Without the trauma of the journey to Laity, he wondered whether he would have arrived in a condition to be open to such acceptance. He said, "At Laity Lodge, no one ever insisted that there was one rigid path to the truth. Always, on every visit, I sensed that I was loved and accepted, regardless of where I was in my journey."

Robert and Lillian Morris

Robert Morris was an outstanding architect in San Antonio. He died suddenly of a heart attack in March 2005. He and his wife, Lillian, first came to Laity Lodge in the 1960s. She wrote, "Our early memories of Laity Lodge bring to mind the sheer beauty of the setting, the rightness of the Great Hall hanging over the Frio River, the dignity and vastness of the canyon, and the humanity of the sign: 'Yes! You do drive in the river!' That's what comes to mind; then there is what comes to the heart—the people: Bill and Betty Ann Cody, Frog Sullivan, Frances Worley, the staff, the campers, and the amazing people who opened up their hearts to us in such personal and alarming ways, while gently leading us to a new openness with each other, with them, and with God.

"We came to Laity and walked, played tennis, swam, threw rocks, sat on chiggers, pondered great questions, told jokes, laughed, and cried. For the most part we were authentic, and the rest of the time acutely aware that we weren't, but that at least we wanted to be.

"There was this freedom not to participate and at the same time, we could see others being strengthened, or threatened, or both, and continuing on the journey of self-discovery and worship that called us to be seekers and self-examiners. It was exciting, sometimes depressing in process, and very real. Everything was immediate; the idea of postponing the work of struggling and living was not an option: we were tinder set aflame.

"We learned to take the ideas, the insights—the sharing—with us and not expect the feelings to come along. The feelings of joy and accomplishment after a season at Laity rewarded us for the hard work, but they seldom arrived home at the same intensity or even in the same form. But we had been prepared for reentry and to reconnect with the community at home. One leader likened the experience to the journey of a man who, coming to a high place, can see where he is going . . . and when he is in a low place, can remember the vision of his destination.

"What else can we say about Laity Lodge? It is where our children experienced adolescence in a supportive community, where we reaffirmed our baptism, confirmation, and marriage vows, and verbalized the partnership between ourselves and the Living God."

Daniel and Carol Love

Daniel Love wrote, "Were it not for the Laity Lodge Youth Camps where my younger sister came to work, I would not have met a co-counselor and friend who would become my wife. That alone would merit honorable mention." He continued, speaking of how he became a minister in the Presbyterian Church. "As I made the transition in calling, Laity Lodge itself became a place of spiritual renewal and refreshment for me. Weekend retreats became critical times to deepen my connection with God and to ask, 'What next?'" He concluded, "Even now I schedule a summer retreat as often as I can to take part in the holistic ministry of Laity Lodge and to catch a sense of the work of the Spirit in our world."

Daniel's wife Carol wrote, "I marvel at God, the Weaver. I'm grateful for the careful push and pull of the loom as new textures are added to the fabric of life. The H. E. Butt Foundation introduced some of the more colorful threads in the changing pattern of my life."

She continued, "If words can make a woven tapestry, these would be some images symbolized by the color Laity Lodge brings to my life.

> Orange: Butterflies in my stomach as I drive in the canyon, anticipating new experiences.
> White: Sneakers, soggy walks in the river, and great conversations with friends.
> Green: Tennis courts, unrivaled best place for a surprise dance.
> Tan: Volleyball court, place to meet a friend through whom I met my husband.
> Blue: River and sky, refreshing re-creation outdoors.
> Yellow: Great Hall, warm rich teaching and worship.
> Red: Feelings, felt strongly in a safe place.
> Purple: Story, privilege of listening to another.
> Brown: Clay, centering creativity.
> Gray: Stone and wood, grounding touch of décor and landscaping.
> Black: Words, Scripture, and other written reflections giving witness to God.

Laity Lodge continues to serve as a place of renewal when I bring my stained and snagged fabric to the canyon."

Jack Willome

Some places seem to be haunted more than others by God's presence. The stars appear to bend down at night. The trees wave to us, and clear, spring water giggles with delight. We are prone to stop more often to see what is around us and take time with tiny white, purple, or pink flowers that raise their gentle heads in nature's garden. Celtic Christians described these places as "thin" because in them, the veil between the Holy One and us sometimes is nearly nonexistent.

While on a retreat at Laity Lodge, a man named Jack began to become awakened. Tall, dark, and handsome, Jack met all of our culture's criteria for the definition of success. In the late 1970s, during his last eighteen months in the army, he filled a financial need by moonlighting as the first accountant for Laity Lodge. While in the army he passed his CPA exam, and following his discharge was hired by a home-building company. In record time, he became the chief financial officer, and by thirty-two years of age was CEO of the largest privately owned home-building company in America.

The price of his success hit him closest to home. This successful businessman was out of touch with his children. He left home before they were awake and returned after they were asleep. He was on the edge of a divorce. He drank too much. He worked seven days a week and was never out of touch with employees who could tell him how many houses were sold that day. The passion that drove him was money.

However, the Hound of Heaven was using the dark side of his success journey. The uneasiness helped him confide in Bill Cody, who urged him to try again with his wife Dee and to get his family into church. Further, Bill said, "Jack, I know enough about you and your family to tell you that getting your family into church is not enough. If you are serious about your marriage, you will be at the couples' retreat at Laity Lodge next weekend."

Wanting information to tell his wife, Jack asked, "Who is leading the retreat?"

Cody replied, "A Catholic priest from Indiana."

Jack was raised in a church that had at least one annual anti-Catholic sermon. Moreover, he had just "made" his family join the church, and now he was asking his wife to go on a retreat led by a priest! What could a priest possibly have to say to anyone about marriage? But they went to the retreat.

At the close of the experience, Jack went to the speaker to tell him how much the retreat had meant. Keith Hosey, the priest, sat down with Jack on a bench just outside the Great Hall. He put his arm on Jack's shoulders and prayed for him. He prayed that the Lord would come into Jack's life and that he would be healed just like Jesus had healed others—healed of his obsession to work, healed of his passion for money, healed of his estrangement from his wife, children, and parents. It was the first time Jack had heard someone pray specifically for him. He wept.

Struggles followed, flashing in Technicolor—but his troubles with family, parents, work, and time priorities no longer devoured his life. Jack found strength through private devotions, his church, a local sharing group, AA, retreats, and a group of young CEOs. The latter group had a monthly conference call. They were all committed to live out their faith through their work, family, and community. The phone conversations focused on each person answering two questions. What is good for you now? Where do you need prayer? Each talked until he shared all he desired and then they prayed. That group has been active for more than fifteen years.

Jack came to have a new understanding of the meaning of the ministry of the laity.[2] While he had been taught that the ministry of the laity meant serving the church as an institution, he also came to see it as the life he was living. One part of this new understanding was seeing his ministry through his work. He sensed God must be included in his decision making and in all relationships on the job, at home with wife and children, with parents, with members of the community, and with everyone in God's very large family.

Jack began to do his homework in earnest. He planned time with his wife, time with his children, and time for all of them to be together as a family. He began the difficult task of exploring the painful parts of his relationships with each of his parents and spent hours in open conversation with each one. He and Dee prayed for the relationship she had with his mother. That reconciliation happened after years of prayer and many hours of often heart-wrenching conversation.

Retreats at Laity Lodge became a major source of refreshment, renewal, rest, and rekindling of personal relationships for Jack and Dee. He was invited to go to Haiti and became acquainted with some businessmen and women there. He followed with annual visits and assisting, at first, seven men in coming to a retreat for business and professionals at Laity Lodge. Each year after that first meeting, they came with their spouses to Laity Lodge. Jack arranged for seven Haitian teenagers to attend the Laity Lodge Youth Camps for a two-week session. The Laity Lodge experience took on an international flavor.

Jack Willome heard and acted on the invitation from Jesus: "Follow me!"

Charles Huffman

Charles "Chuck" Huffman told the story of the impact his church's annual Laity Lodge retreats made on him and the church. He said, "I discovered Laity Lodge in 1967 when I was beginning my ordained ministry at St. David's Episcopal Church in Austin, Texas. There I was blessed to begin a friendship with Keith Miller, who had just left Laity Lodge as its first director to pursue graduate studies at the University of Texas." Chuck and Keith began lay-renewal programs, encouraged by the obvious hunger of those attending to take their faith on a deeper spiritual journey.

Chuck said, "Those days were a time to integrate what I had just learned at Seminary with what I was learning about parish life and, in particular, about the role of the laity in the Church. I came to appreciate the power of personal witnessing, and the capacity of small groups to help transform casual Christians into energized disciples and members of the Community."

In July 1968, Chuck and his wife Carolyn attended their first Summer Institute of Lay Studies at Laity Lodge. Chuck thought at the time, "Two Episcopalians and two Southern Baptists, speaking with one voice—what a novel idea in a culture where attitudes of exclusivism and sectarianism were all too common!" The leaders' commitment to Jesus Christ, the quality and authority of their teaching, the openness and warmth of the participants, the beauty of the Frio Canyon, the ingenious architecture, the quality of the facilities, plus all the amenities of the program, left Chuck's soul thirsting for more of Laity Lodge.

Chuck and Carolyn attended another conference the following June. Then, with evangelical fervor, they convinced six other members of St. David's that the joys awaiting them at Laity were well worth the sacrifice of six precious days of their vacations. Overcoming the reluctance that Episcopalians often have about attending a religious conference, especially one sponsored by a Southern Baptist family, was no small challenge. Of course, Chuck knew they would discover, as he had, that Laity Lodge was not religious in any traditional sense of the word, and that any fear they had about having to guard against a rigid or fundamentalist program was an illusion. "Trust us, you won't be sorry," Chuck told them. He added, "They did, and they weren't! I gained great pleasure in giving this gift to those who came, a pleasure I still receive whenever I can convince a stranger to risk the Laity Lodge adventure."

In the summer of 1969, Chuck and Carolyn took a week of vacation to attend another conference of the Institute of Lay Studies at Laity Lodge. This time, their three daughters enrolled in the Laity Lodge Youth Camps. Once again, Chuck left Laity feeling motivated, inspired, and excited about the church leadership role he was just beginning.

In 1973, Chuck was called to be the rector of St. Matthew's Episcopal Church in Austin. "It was natural that Laity Lodge would become an important asset by which my congregation and I would grow as a Christian Community." St. Matthew's had its first parish weekend at Laity in the spring of 1974. Every year since, sixty to seventy members from St. Matthew's have attended a spring weekend retreat.

Chuck passed along to me his insights into church growth and the role Laity Lodge played in the lives of new members. As every church leader knows, any new member who does not quickly establish a relationship with another church member will probably slip through the back door. As soon as possible at St. Matthew's, Chuck tried to get new people into groups and encouraged them to participate in other parish functions. Chuck said, "Nothing has been more effective than the annual Laity Lodge Weekend to facilitate the bonding between new and old members."

He continued, "Laity Lodge is a kind of jump-start experience in bonding, to help new members or unconnected members rapidly feel a part of the Community. The hope and reality is that back in the parish, those who participated in a weekend will build on their new relationships and contribute to the ministry and mission of parish life."

In addition to community building, Laity Lodge provided a solid and helpful venue for learning about the Christian faith. The speakers at a Laity Lodge weekend were always theologically sound and skillful communicators. Chuck said, "The director collaborates with the pastor to find the right speakers for each parish. Sometimes leaders are selected from the same denomination, but, as often as not, they come from another background." Their different perspectives and approaches proved to be healthy and provocative to the understanding of our faith and to the dispelling of prejudices.

Another important means used by Laity Lodge for communicating the practical concerns of the Christian life was lay witnessing. Chuck said, "Those of us in traditions that have stressed an extensive education for their clergy have not always been comfortable allowing lay people to share spiritual insights publicly—aside from the fact that the Bible enjoins every Christian to do precisely this. (See 1 Peter 3:15.)" At Laity Lodge, non-professional, theologically untrained witnesses often communicated with credible freshness and unavoidable truth.

Also important was how small groups at Laity Lodge provided an experience that further encouraged participation in such groups back home. The groups built a healthy, solid support base for the Body of Christ.

Chuck said, "Laity Lodge was an ideal place for spiritual refreshment and inspiration. Just sitting in a swing or on a rock in a picture-perfect, Texas Hill Country setting was nourishment for the soul. Over the years Laity Lodge has been all that and more for the members of St. Matthew's. It has become a long-term partnership." Chuck's church and Laity Lodge continue to work together as the Bible says in Ephesians 4:12: "to equip the saints for the work of ministry, for building up the body of Christ" (ESV).

Chuck concluded with a note shared by thousands of people whose lives have been changed at Laity Lodge, "We offer our deepest thanks to Howard Butt, Jr., his family, and all the staff and resources of the H. E. Butt Foundation."

Notes

1 All the stories in this chapter are used by permission.

2 Jack Willome recommends the following books on this subject: *The Velvet Covered Brick* and *Renewing America's Soul* by Howard Butt, *The Soul of the Firm* by Bill Pollard,

Loving Monday by John Beckett, *Your Work Matters to God* by Sherman and Hendricks, *Maximize Your Ministry* by Robert Slocum, *Business as a Calling* by Michael Novak, *A Theology of the Laity* by Hendrik Kraemer, *Good Intentions Aside* and *Church on Sunday, Work on Monday* by Laura Nash, and *The Working Life* by Joanne B. Ciulla.

Chapter 10

The Future of the Dream

Transition

Because the church is a living organism and the Spirit of God is not predictable, the shape of the ministry of the church is surprising and varied. When Jesus was with his followers, living his life and teaching what his life implied, he provided glimpses of the future church. His church would heal the sick, respect every person, lead by serving, give generously, love graciously and inclusively, teach truth, seek ways to honor others, transform the culture (by outlawing slavery and child labor, for example), and develop peacemakers.

Since I retired in 1999, Laity Lodge has continued its many activities and also developed in exciting ways. Through the Department of Racial and Ethnic Ministries of the Baptist General Convention of Texas, forty couples representing twenty-seven language groups met at Laity Lodge in their first annual retreat.

Earlier I mentioned the ministry of Jack Willome and the gathering of Christian leaders from Haiti and children from there who have attended the youth camps.

Crane Scholars from Baylor University, brilliant students who will be attending graduate school at MIT, Oxford, Yale, Harvard, Cambridge, Stanford, and other excellent universities, now come to Laity Lodge to explore the relationship between their faith and their chosen vocations.

New professors from Baylor attend a pre-school retreat to explore the relationship of their faith to the subjects they teach and further explore how faith relates to the classroom.

The Chrysostom Society, a highly regarded group of Christian writers, has met at Laity Lodge and written for Laity Lodge publications. Each year, one society member spends a month at Laity as writer in residence, writing and speaking at several weekend retreats. Madeleine L'Engle, author of *A Wrinkle in Time* and more than fifty-five other books, was one of the first to establish this tradition. Her time at Laity Lodge was so important to her that she scheduled her speaking engagements around her stay.

Plans for artists, writers, musicians, and theologians to be in residence at Laity Lodge for longer periods are being expanded. Facilities designed for this purpose have been built. Retreats for visual and performing artists and musicians are also projected, aimed at audiences both at Laity Lodge and the Laity Lodge Youth Camps. The Cody Center art gallery features a new artist each quarter from a broad spectrum of the art world. This continues to have an ever-widening scope.

Don Murdock, executive director of Laity Lodge (1997–2006), sought to provide a global perspective in line with our vision statement: "That God may be glorified and the nations come to faith." Murdock explained, "To sustain Laity Lodge's commitment to the larger world, Howard Butt Jr. has always focused Laity's energy within the smaller circle of influence . . . that is, the people and institutions with which it is possible to have a personal relationship. Laity Lodge is not only a safe place for the strugglers, stragglers, doubters, sinners, and cynics, it is fundamentally a community of relationships willing to befriend anyone God sends its way." We help people grow in faith, move from darkness into light, and transform their lives at retreats. As one of Laity's speakers, Bill Pannell of Fuller Theological Seminary, said, "Laity Lodge is very subversive, very countercultural, a prophetic movement within and outside the church to which it is also devoted."

Don Murdock spoke to the heart of Laity Lodge's purpose: "Laity Lodge at its best helps people understand and embrace God's call to be in this world as Christ's people and to be instruments to transform culture rather than living apart from it or letting our culture transform us into its image of how people ought to be in the world."

Don died in March 2006. At his memorial service, people shared many stories about how Don himself embraced God's call. He transformed the culture of Laity Lodge, and for that we will always be grateful. His words still remind us, "Laity Lodge's passion for renewal of our world must be prayerfully protected and nurtured. As Laity takes care of this fundamental work, there's every reason to believe that God will be faithful in revealing wise global strategies that will free Laity Lodge to do its best on behalf of its mission to all the nations."

The Future[1]

Bible words like "cities" and "nations" speak of more than geography. They speak of the human social need for organizations. They speak of institutions. Schools, companies, clubs, hospitals, unions, teams, political parties, governments—all these are included in the Scripture's immense emphasis on "the city" and "the nation." How does the gospel change the way we function in our institutions? Exploring this question will be basic to Laity Lodge's future.

Laity Lodge has developed over the years by remaining open to the moment. Changes in direction always emerge from within the fabric of what we are doing currently. So it is impossible to think about Laity Lodge's future without reviewing its past. Howard Butt Jr. said, "One of the great gratitudes of my life is the way we have been a part of the enormous resurgence in the church as the potential of the laity—the depth and power of the calling of the laity—has opened in the last forty-five years." This priesthood of all believers is obvious in the New Testament, but it began in the Old Testament with the vision given to Moses. Gradually, the church today is recovering this vision through the help of Laity Lodge and similar organizations.

Elton Trueblood said at Laity Lodge's first retreat that we were gathered here as a part of the continuing reformation. This reformation has been moving ahead at a remarkable speed over the forty-five years Laity Lodge has been in operation. More and more people are beginning to understand Elton Trueblood's vision of the great commission. When Jesus told us, "Go into all the worlds and preach the gospel," he did not mean that just geographically, but vocationally. He didn't mean just preach the gospel in Africa, China, or Japan. He meant go into the world of business and preach the gospel. Go into the world of homemaking and law and aeronautics and electronics and preach the gospel. Go into all the worlds . . . and preach the gospel by the way you live your life.

As Laity Lodge looks ahead, we see a continuation of experiences of authenticity and empowerment. Laity Lodge will continue to be a source of inspiration for different kinds of people, a springboard for them to take their experiences back into the world. Laity Lodge represents an ageless truth about the whole calling of the whole people of God.

One main reason for the anointing presence of God here is that Laity Lodge represents something of a part of God's historic revelation to humanity. Laity Lodge reveals and brings out the potential, the plan, the ministry He has for each human life. People come to Laity Lodge and take part of it home with them. The Laity Lodge experience is not confined to the picturesque banks of the Frio. The authentic experience is God Himself. God empowers the lives of the guests for the specific and individual communication of the spiritual reality, as each guest goes home to experience God in kitchens, offices, clubs, parties, schoolrooms, sports fields. The work of God takes place in the world.

Laity Lodge has plugged into something that the church is gradually rediscovering: a vision of the totality of the people of God working for the totality of our lives in the ordinary affairs of life. The institutional church exists for teaching and equipping and empowering the people of God, but the work of the kingdom takes place out in the secular world. This notion is the non-negotiable part of Laity Lodge's future. The tools, techniques, and methods will unfold through the staff and the guests. They will continue to be a powerful part of determining Laity Lodge's past, present, and future.

Howard Butt Jr. has sought to translate the Christian faith into everyday life since he began his work as a college student. He continued in his path of Christian service while he worked in the grocery business. Upon the building and development of Laity Lodge, Howard devoted himself to laity renewal full time.

In many ways, Laity Lodge is the best-kept secret in Texas, which is both a positive and negative observation. As we move into the future, we don't want to keep such a positive experience a secret. Each director has built remarkable relationships with churches and lay leadership all over Texas and America, and future directors will continue to develop relationships. Howard Butt Jr. is known as a bridge builder, and his daughter Deborah and her husband David Rogers, vice president of the H. E. Butt Foundation, are building a bridge between the older generation that has known and loved Laity Lodge and the next generation just beginning to know it. Laity Lodge witnesses to a generational faith, implicit in a God revealed as Triunity—Father, Son, and Spirit, Three in One.

Bridging the generations for Laity Lodge retreats is only part of the task for the future. Clergy and lay leadership have changed. The Butt family hopes to place an emphasis on making sure Laity Lodge is a vital part of the churches it works with—integrating Laity Lodge into the hearts of these churches, not just providing another retreat. They look for those pastors who share a vision of empowering the laity.

Recently, many organizations have begun grappling with faith in daily life. The Coalition for Ministry in Daily Life and the Yale Center for Faith and Culture are two ecumenical examples. There has also been a recent proliferation of books in this field. In the future, Laity Lodge may provide a place for these different organizations to convene. It has already developed a national reputation for bringing together different denominations and strands of Christianity. Laity Lodge hopes to encourage organizations focused on faith in daily life by pulling them together and offering a place to meet.

Another part of the future of Laity Lodge is to spread out the base of people who understand the importance of empowering the laity. We desire to mobilize people with a deep commitment to this vision. Over the last several decades "the priesthood of all believers" has gained wider acceptance, and we hope to increase this understanding ever further.

A major change has occurred in seminaries since Laity Lodge's inception. When, in the 1940s, Howard Butt Jr. wanted to study theology on a non-ordination track, he was something of an anomaly. He had to be interviewed all the way up to the seminary president to be admitted to study theology as a layperson. Now many denominations include special programs in their seminaries designed for the laypeople who want to study theology but don't want to be ordained. They are beginning to understand the importance of equipping the laity for work in the kingdom. Because of these changes, Howard Butt Jr. believes, "The best days of Laity Lodge are ahead." Revival is gaining momentum as it did in the 1940s youth revival. Bruce McIver told the story of the youth revival movement in his recent book *Riding the Wind of God.* Since its beginnings, Laity Lodge has been "riding the wind of God" and will continue to revive and empower the laity.

David Rogers's expanding leadership role also excites Howard. "David is a remarkable man," he says, "with gifts that far exceed my own in many ways." The forty-five years of family guidance has provided a rich foundation for Laity Lodge. Howard's mother first entrusted Laity Lodge to him "to implement his vision, as a tool in his hands." Since then, he has devoted much of his life to the work in the canyon and beyond. Both Mrs. Butt and Howard Jr.'s lives embodied the remarkable effectiveness Christian laypeople can achieve. Howard Jr. bought into his parent's vision of service, and David and Deborah have bought into that same vision. As the next generation of leadership, they typify Laity Lodge's emphasis on family renewal.

David Rogers sees several challenges as Laity Lodge moves ahead. Oswald Chambers wrote, "The need is never the call: the need is the opportunity."[2] People come to David with all kinds of ideas and opportunities for retreats, many wonderful ideas. His challenge is to filter these ideas through Laity Lodge's mission and to select those retreats where our ministry can be most productive. David said, "We will develop our strengths and focus on our mission because, realistically, we cannot do everything."

David is also excited about bringing a new generation to Laity Lodge. Of course, he recognizes the challenge of doing so. Society has changed since the days of those first retreats. Some parents today won't take a weekend away from their kids because they don't want to miss a single soccer game. Often both spouses work full-time—a huge difference from those couples who first came to Laity Lodge. Since families now have less time together, many of them are hesitant to give up a weekend for the parents to attend a spiritual retreat. Competition in the travel industry gives families even more reasons to avoid a spiritual retreat. Why spend time and money and effort traveling to Leakey,

Texas, when the family could take an inexpensive cruise or a quick Cancun vacation? The temptation now is to whisk the family away on a ready-made and simple vacation.

Many young parents today run at an incredibly fast pace in society. The idea of slowing down doesn't compute—until they do it. Then they see the value in it. They don't recognize the hectic pace of modern life and the cacophony of sounds that assault us until they spend a weekend in quiet reflection. Getting away is more crucial now than ever before because our world moves so fast.

At the first retreat at Laity Lodge, Howard Butt Jr. said, "We retreat to move forward." That's what prayer teaches us in our personal lives: We turn aside and retreat to serenity and meditation so that we can move forward, empowered for the tasks that are ours. Retreats also help us discern which tasks are ours. Surrounded by busy crowded cities and traffic jams and blaring horns and schedules always running behind, bombarded with noise from cell phones and voice mail, with communication on the Internet, e-mail, instant messaging, text messaging, blogging, even the old school cable TV and radio—many people don't even realize how desperate they are. They need a place where the pace slows down, a place of quiet and freedom. Laity Lodge is such a place.

David is also excited to find the right balance of speakers for each retreat. Laity Lodge is an ecumenical retreat center that seeks to present cutting-edge speakers. These speakers need to be sound theologically without being focused on denominational issues. In the past, nationally known speakers have had personal relationships with Howard Butt Jr. or with the directors. These speakers believed in the powerful work of Laity Lodge. More and more, however, nationally known speakers are accustomed to addressing thousands of people at a time. They receive enormous honoraria for a two-hour stint. They fly in and out alone. Many of them have never experienced a speaking engagement like Laity Lodge, where they learn the names of all seventy-two people at the retreat, where they have several days to explore an idea in much greater depth and with raw honesty, where they bring their spouses and find themselves as refreshed and revived as the guests.

Well-known speakers will continue to make room in their busy schedules. Many of them will continue to speak at Laity Lodge because they will fall in love with it. Our staff will continue to build relationships with speakers in a way that is true to the historic faith, but still fresh and contemporary. Laity Lodge is committed to integrating faith and daily life. However, finding the best speakers—and fitting their busy schedules into Laity's schedule—will remain a continuing challenge.

David knows there is one thing about the future that will not be a challenge. Howard and Barbara Dan have not set up parameters. They have passed the family's philosophy and vision to David and Deborah and freed them to do what God leads them to do. Howard knows Laity Lodge will face challenges in the future that he can't envision. He trusts Deborah and David to carry on with God's guidance. "With David's gifts," Howard Butt said recently, "Laity Lodge will be increasingly productive and strategic."

Laity Lodge has grown through the past forty-five years because it has God's anointing. The Butt family has simply tried to follow God's will step by step as He showed the path to them. At a retreat several years ago, Howard Butt Jr. shared the vision of Laity Lodge once again. "I don't know what pain and anguish and grief you may be in at this moment in your life," he told the guests. "But I do know this: the power that we experience here—and that we can experience everywhere—is the resurrection power of Jesus Christ." The vision of Laity Lodge is no larger than the vision of Jesus Christ. And no smaller. Laity Lodge will continue to share the promise Jesus made to all Christians in John 10:10: "I came so they can have real and eternal life, more and better life than they ever dreamed of" (*The Message*).

Notes

1 This information was taken from an interview with Howard Butt Jr., on July 13, 2005, and used with permission.

2 Oswald Chambers, "Is He Really Lord?," *My Utmost for His Highest* (New York: Dodd, Mead and Co., 1935), devotion for March 5.

Appendix A: Poetry and Music

Poem

A lawyer pled in tired tones,
please tell us of the seeds we've sown,
That there is life in what we've done,
with all the hours of the race we've run.
A student well past thirty years,
is back in school amidst his fears.
That time has flown far too fast,
he found no meaning in life that's past.
He wants to know if this is all
he can expect from life so small?
"Perhaps in learning? I want to find,
a way of life, different in kind,
Than what I've known up to now.
I'll leave it all, and take my bow,
And leave this world, this barren land,
diploma earned, my cap in hand.
I'll ask some soul if he could tell,
of more than some dark wishing well.
Perhaps a child, lost in play,
could help me find a fuller way.
At least I've heard a rumor tell."
And Jesus knew it very well. (HH)

Breaking Down Fences

The world is made of pastures green, and fields for life that always seem
Far better there. So I'll go hence, in search of life beyond the fence
Of my small world, my work, my town, my family, my church, the sound,
Of neighbors near, and common days. I'll find real life, in brand new ways.
What will it take to get me there? Where I can breathe some different air
Than all the folks in my small town. I'll crash the fence. Break it down!
Trying to stop a ladder man from leaving life where it began,
And scaling all, up to the top, of barren ways and balloons that pop.
He'll find a life that's lined with gold and papered thin with green that's cold.
The years have gone, and now he's old. Where is the life he found he'd sold?
He's taking time to see again, the pastures green where once he'd been.
And there was God, and family too, and caring neighbors, work to do,
Love and joy, and all he'd sought, all the things that can't be bought.
(HH)

Psalm

From past generations we take in a burden of shame.
From our families we wrongly learn we are faultily made.
From all shame, O Lord, free us.
From our own decisions we have experienced guilt.
Our choices, our own choices, have weighted our hearts.
From real guilt, O Lord, deliver us. (HH)

Altars Everywhere

Through the days in Mystery's ways,
Work is done by everyone.
Children's play is heaven's way
Altars there are everywhere.

Trees and faces show God's graces.
Ants and dogs and big green frogs,
Water clear, and stars so near,
Altars there are everywhere.

At the school in breezes cool,
Teachers near and friendships dear,
Playing games and PC frames,
Altars there are everywhere.

Reaching teens and fears extremes,
Cars and dates and lifting weights,
Hold a dream to make some team,
Altars there are everywhere.

Find your work and get a perk
Get a spouse and buy a house.
Business cards and larger yards.
Altars there are everywhere.

Children come and everyone,
Gift unique, God's awesome feat,
Parents bear, love's burdens fair,
Altars there are everywhere.

Questions rise with some surprise.
What's life for? There must be more?
Meaning find, the final kind,
Altars there are everywhere.

There's a Fall, God bears it all.
Love so great, our hearts remake,
Heaven's smile, draws each child,
Altars there are in Christ's care. (HH)

Laity

The power of God can best be known,
Through daily work, a loving home,
Common worship and private prayer.
Christ's own Spirit dwelling there.

A listening ear and generous sharing,
Time for others, God's own caring.
Our work place then becomes an altar—
Makes God known and evil falter. (HH)

Appendix B:
Small-group Facilitator

Welcome to the Team

We are grateful for your willingness to serve as a facilitator. This booklet is intended as a guide and source of ideas to assist you as a facilitator. Choose those items you think will be helpful to you. You are always welcome and encouraged to talk to the Laity Lodge retreat director about any concerns you have.

Please plan to arrive at Laity Lodge by 5:00 p.m. so you can settle into your room and be at the team meeting by 6:00. This will give us time to meet each other, get a feel for the retreat, talk over the small-group process, and pray.

Basic Philosophy of Laity Lodge

The purpose of Laity Lodge is the renewal of society through the renewal of the church, family, and individuals. The primary goal is to provide a place where individuals can be free to be vulnerable and explore options that can lead to a deeper relationship with God. Each person who comes to Laity Lodge, in Jesus Christ, is loved and accepted just as they are. The focus of all that Laity Lodge does is on Jesus Christ, the Scriptures, and healthy relationships with God, our families, church, society, ourselves, and others. Nutrition and exercise are basic parts of each retreat and will be expressed in the meals served, facilities available, and sufficient time for exercise. Beauty and excellence are also Laity Lodge values. The schedule will be relaxed and unhurried. There will be time for small groups as well. We recommend eight to ten and a maximum of twelve in a group.

Purpose of Small Groups

Provide a safe, confidential place for personal sharing.

Assist in the application of the Bible and our relationship with God to all aspects of life.

Encourage a deeper personal commitment to Christ.

Receive and give love, acceptance, and support.

Experience prayer.

Process information, especially that which is provided by the speakers.

Explore tensions between Christian and cultural values. Create a safe environment to discuss these tensions.

Offer a genuine experience of Christian community. Often it is a person's first such experience.

Function of the Small-group Facilitator

To listen!

To enjoy the group.

To invite each person to enjoy the group, to participate however they wish, to be silent if that is their choice. A quiet listener is still participating.

To encourage dialogue between participants. We learn from each other.

To be open, honest, loving.

To keep the group focused on the practical and personal, not theoretic; on sharing and not answers.

To provide the most conducive physical setting, comfortable with good eye contact.

To provide whatever structure the group needs.

To protect the group from a talkative, dominating person.

To make sure everyone has an opportunity to speak.

To listen! Pay full attention to each person.

Guidelines

Confidentiality—what is said in the room will stay in the room.

Speak for self—not for someone else in the group or outside the group. We do not tell another (or the whole group) what they should think, feel, or do.

Mutual respect—this is not an answer-giving time, but rather a time to explore. Allow each person to make their own decisions regarding participation. Each has something to contribute and to receive.

How to Begin

Think of group experiences you have had and what gave you a sense of welcome, trust, and expectancy.

Welcome the group. If it seems to fit, have a brief prayer. Sometimes the group flows from the beginning, and a specific prayer time may not be needed.

Identify the guidelines. (Brief, yet clear.)

Have individuals introduce themselves if they are willing. One way to do this is to ask, "What would you like to tell us so we could know you just a bit better?" Or, "Let's each share one thing that's been especially good for us this year." Or, "What spoke to you during this morning's session?"

You may have limited time. That is fine. At times the process may not go very deep. God can work with that. Therefore don't try to make something happen. Let go and let God take care of that.

Remember, some of the people in the group will be in a good place. Acknowledge and celebrate the good.

You may want to invite each person to participate or not to participate as they choose. You might say something like, "Some of you may not feel like talking. That's fine; listening is a gift."

Begin with yourself (briefly and to the point, as this becomes a model for others). Do this on a personal level with your own joys and your concerns. If you share on a personal level, they will sense a trust level in the group.

Leadership Skills

Ask God to help you see each person as He does. This will help you listen with your heart and will help you give your careful attention to the person who is speaking. Behold the person.

Hospitality—be a good host: create a welcoming environment, where everyone has eye contact with everyone else, especially the leader. Minimize distracting noise. Greet each person by name.

Pay careful attention to each person through eye contact, relaxed but engaged body language, and listening, listening, listening to what the person is actually saying. Remember, each person is the authority on what they said.

Enhance communication through:

> Clarifying what was said.
>
> Paraphrasing what was said.
>
> Encouraging each person to speak for self, using "I" messages.
>
> Asking open-ended questions for more information regarding feelings, thoughts, beliefs.
>
> Encouraging concreteness—clear, simple statements of a person's actual experience, thoughts, feelings. Avoid getting sidetracked on theoretical issues.

Be concrete yourself.

Be genuine—open to share your own ideas, feelings, experiences, not as answers but as modeling and mutuality. It is important to remember that the group members are helped most when each individual comes up with his/her own answers. Be free to respond to others naturally.

Be respectful by allowing each person to participate or not participate at their level and by their choice.

Facilitate conversation across the group, encouraging people to talk to each other.

If things get quiet, do not feel that you have to do something to "get everyone talking." God may want to reach each person through silence.

Demonstrate kindness and compassion.

Listen, listen, listen. Listen especially to God, and then to each person.

In short, a competent, skilled small group leader is Caring—Congruent—Concrete.

Difficult Group Members

Person talks too much . . .

Person with all the answers and/or is very preachy . . .

One way to deal with such a person is to say, "I sense this is very important to you; we can come back to that." Or, "Let's make a time and talk this over after lunch." Gently but firmly move the conversation to another person. If there is more than one session, suggest to the person between sessions a way he/she can be more supportive to the process. Remind them that this is a time for caring—not for curing.

Characteristics of good questions to ask the group

Clear and simple.

Can be answered briefly.

Does not require people to "confess their sins."

Can be answered by every member in the group.

Will help the group to know each other better.

Is worth the time for the group members.

Does not require a "yes" or "no" answer.

Allows for each member to answer in a different way.

Relates to the material at hand.

Encourages discussion of real issues in that person's life.

Prayer and the Small Group

Often prayer is appropriate at the beginning and/or end. Not always. Do not feel there has to be a prayer time. Usually it will be natural to pray.

Prayer causes us not only to talk about God but to talk with God.

Prayer is an indicator that God is the real teacher and presence in a group.

Praying out loud is threatening for some and, therefore, difficult or impossible. Give people the freedom to decline.

Some Ways Prayers May Be Offered in a Group
The facilitator prays.
Invite volunteers to give a word or sentence prayer.
Hold hands in a circle or huddle and invite volunteers to pray.
A word of caution about long prayers may be necessary.
Sit in silent prayer.
Have a conversational prayer.
Call out the person's name and all pray in silence for that person.
Ask each person how the group, or the person on their left, could best
    pray for them.
Covenant to pray for one person (or each person in the group) during
    the retreat and/or during the week following.
Have a time of prayer centered on thanks.

Laity Lodge

Laity Lodge is dedicated to our desire to know Christ, and what that
means in the ordinary, everyday places and relationships of our lives. It
is a place where, in a safe, quiet, environment, the laity can explore
choices leading to growth—in creativity, effectiveness, and fulfillment.
It seeks to implement the values of excellence, service, and unity.
Spiritual vitality, educational innovation, and organizational excite-
ment have characterized Laity Lodge since its inception.

(Barry Sweet developed a small-group facilitator booklet from material
Roberta Hestenes taught at Fuller Seminary, and David Williamson
refined it to create this edition.)

Appendix C: H. E. Butt Foundation and the Laity Lodge Foundation

Motto
The renewal of society through the renewal of the Church; Church renewal through renewal of the family; family renewal through renewed individuals.

Vision Statement
So that God may be glorified and the nations come to faith . . . our vision is to equip believers in Jesus Christ to practice servant leadership as modeled by the Holy Trinity to renew ourselves, families, institutions, and society.

Beliefs
1. Centrality of Jesus Christ

2. Authority of the Scripture

3. Scripture and a sound psychological understanding are mutually complementary

4. "Priesthood of all believers" means that the laity has responsibility for ministry

5. Relationships full of Christ's love express the Scattered Church.

6. Generational healing.

Values

1. To practice **excellence** in all that we do

2. To provide **a safe place** where individuals can be free from an agenda

3. To value **music and art** as expressions of the Spirit of God

4. To see **humor, laughter, and fun** as important expressions of joy

5. To support and encourage **local congregations and their clergy**

6. To **model vulnerability** with open sharing of the truth about our lives

7. To pursue an **evangelical vision** implemented in **ecumenical breadth**

8. To seek **human unity—through relational reconciliation**—as the expression of Triune unity

9. To practice **relational sensitivity**—meeting people where they are—in our lives and in our programs

10. To recognize the **giftedness of each staff member** as critical to our effectiveness

11. To **serve one another in love**

12. To commit ourselves to sustaining **long-term relationships**

13. To practice **intellectual integrity and responsibility**

14. To pursue **inclusiveness**

15. To cultivate **reflective spiritual discernment**

16. To place **high value on the family**

17. To respect **privacy** and the **dignity of the individual**

18. To be **good stewards** of all our **human, natural, and financial resources**

Mission Statements

LAITY LODGE, a Christian retreat center, is dedicated to our common quest to know Christ and what that means in the ordinary secular relationships of our lives. It is a place where people are free to explore choices leading to growth in creativity, effectiveness, and servant leadership.

LAITY LODGE YOUTH CAMP is a coed, interdenominational Christian youth camp focusing on spontaneity, fun, and relationships to show kids the best two weeks of their lives, while sharing with them the gospel message and love of Jesus Christ. LLYC is dedicated to providing campers with healthy fun in an emotionally safe learning environment.

FOUNDATION FREE CAMPS provide free camping facilities for qualified church and community-service groups. The program especially targets children and youth groups in Texas communities who would not otherwise be able to afford such an experience. The goal is to provide a place conducive to healthy Christian character development.

Appendix D:
Some of My Favorite Books

A

A Guide to Prayer (Upper Room)
Alcoholics Anonymous
St. Augustine, *The Confessions*

B

Hans Urs von Balthasar, *Prayer*
Karl Barth, *Evangelical Theology: An Introduction*
St. Benedict, *The Rule of St. Benedict*
Peter Berger, A *Rumor of Angels*
Anthony Bloom, *Beginning to Pray*
Roberta Bondi, *Memories of God, In Ordinary Time*
Dietrich Bonhoeffer, *Life Together, Ethics, The Cost of Discipleship*
John Bradshaw, *Bradshaw On: The Family, Healing the Shame that Binds*
Dale Bruner, *The Christbook, The Churchbook, The Holy Spirit—Shy Member of the Trinity*
Martin Buber, *I And Thou*
Frederick Buechner, *Speak What We Feel, The Hungering Dark, The Magnificent Defeat, Telling Secrets, The Son Of Laughter, Brendan, Peculiar Treasures, A Room Called Remember, The Sacred Journey*
Bob Buford, *Half-time, Game Plan*
John Bunyan, *Pilgrim's Progress*
Howard Butt, *Who Can You Trust?, The Velvet Covered Brick, Renewing America's Soul*

C

John Calvin, *Institutes of the Christian Religion*
Joanne Ciulla, *The Working Life*
Oswald Chambers, *My Utmost for His Highest*
G. K. Chesterton, *Saint Francis of Assisi, Saint Thomas Aquinas*
John Claypool, *Tracks of a Fellow Struggler, Stories Jesus Still Tells, The
    Divine Alchemist, The Hopeful Heart*
Charles Colson, *Kingdoms in Conflict*
Frank Conroy, *Body and Soul*

D

Paula D'Arcy, *Song for Sarah, A New Set of Eyes, Seeking with All My
    Heart, Sacred Threshold, When People Grieve*
Max De Pree, *Leadership Is an Art*
Francis de Sales, *An Introduction to the Devout Life*
William Diehl, *Thank God, It's Monday*
John Donne, *Prayers*
Fyodor Dostoevsky, *The Brothers Karamazov*

E

Jonathan Edwards, The *Religious Affections*
The Episcopal Prayer Book

F

Harry Fosdick, *Dear Mr. Brown, The Meaning of Prayer*
Edwin Friedman, *Generation to Generation*

G

Mark Gibbs, *Christians with Secular Power*
Romano Guardini, *The Lord*
Os Guinness, *Winning Back the Soul of American Business*

H

Hal Haralson, *Gentle Mercies*
Khaled Hassini, *The Kite Runner*

Baron Friedrich von Hugel, *Selected Letters*
Victor Hugo, *Les Miserables*

I

St. Ignatius, *The Spiritual Exercises of St. Ignatius of Loyola*

J

St. John of the Cross, *The Collected Works of St. John of the Cross*

K

Thomas Kempis, *The Imitation of Christ*
Tracy Kidder, *Mountains Beyond Mountains*
Soren Kierkegaard, *Works of Love, Purity of Heart*
John Killinger, *Beginning Prayer*
Hendrik Kraemer, A *Theology of the Laity*
Hans Kung, *The Catholic Church: A Short History, Great Christian Thinkers*

L

Anne Lamott, *Traveling Mercies*
William Law, *A Serious Call to a Devout and Holy Life*
Brother Lawrence, *The Practice of the Presence of God*
C. S. Lewis, *Mere Christianity, The Screwtape Letters, The Chronicles of Narnia, Space Trilogy, The Weight of Glory, The Four Loves, Letters to Malcolm, Reflections on the Psalms, Till We Have Faces*
Mark Link, *You: Prayer for Beginners and Those Who Have Forgotten How*
Martin Luther, *Commentary on Romans, Galatians*

M

George MacDonald, *The Baronet's Song, The Curate's Awakening*
Brian McLaren, *A Generous Orthodoxy*
Thomas Merton, The *Seven Storey Mountain, New Seeds of Contemplation, No Man Is an Island, Through the Year with Thomas Merton*

Jeanie Miley, *Ancient Psalms for Contemporary Pilgrims, Creative Silence, Becoming Fire, Shared Splendor*
Andrea Miller, *The Eternal Present*
Keith Miller, *The Taste of New Wine*
Malcolm Muggeridge, *Jesus Rediscovered*

N

Napier and Whitaker, *The Family Crucible*
Laura Nash, *Good Intentions Aside*
Armand Nicholi, *The Question of God*
Reinhold Niebuhr, *The Nature and Destiny of Man*
Richard Niebuhr, *Christ and Culture*
Kathleen Norris, *Dakota, the Cloister Walk*
Henri Nouwen, *The Life of the Beloved, In the Name of Jesus, The Wounded Healer, Reaching Out*
Michael Novak, *Business as a Calling*

O

The Oxford Book of Prayers

P, Q

Blaise Pascal, *Pensees*
Eugene Peterson, *Christ Plays in Ten Thousand Places, The Message*
John Piper, *Desiring God*
John Polkinghorne, *Quarks, Chaos and Christianity*
Reynolds Price, *A Serious Way of Wondering*

R

Gerhard von Rad, *Genesis, God at Work in Israel*
David Redding, *Jesus Makes Me Laugh with Him, Prayers I Love, A Rose Will Grow Anywhere, Getting Through the Night*
Francine Rivers, *Redeeming Love*
J. M. Roberts, *The Triumph of the West*
Betsy Rockwood, *A Wide Place for My Steps, When Prayers Are Not Answered*

Richard Rohr, *Everything Belongs, Adam's Return, Jesus' Plan for a New World*
Ronald Rolheiser, *The Holy Longing*

S
Sherman and Hendricks, *Your Work Matters to God*
Robert Slocum, *Maximize Your Ministry*
Fred Smith, *You and Your Network*
Rodney Stark, *The Victory of Reason*

T
Barbara Brown Taylor, *When God Is Silent*
William Temple, *Nature, Man and God*
St. Teresa of Avila, *The Interior Castle*
Eckhart Tolle, *The Power of Now*
Leo Tolstoy, *Reconciliation, The Confessions, War and Peace*
Paul Tournier, *The Meaning of Persons, To Understand Each Other*
A. W. Tozer, *The Pursuit of God*

U, V, W
Evelyn Underhill, *Mysticism, The Spiritual Life, The Collected Papers*
Macrina Wiederkehr, *A Tree Full of Angels, Seasons of Your Heart*
Dallas Willard, *The Divine Conspiracy*

X, Y, Z
Philip Yancey, *Soul Survivor*